The Mother's Book of Well-Being

The Mother's Book of Well-Being

*Caring for yourself
so you can care
for your baby*

Lisa Groen Braner

Conari Press

Cover Design: Kathleen Fivel
Book Design: Maxine Ressler
Author Photo: Roger W. Braner Jr.

Library of Congress Cataloging-in-Publication Data

Braner, Lisa Groen.
  The mother's book of well-being : caring for yourself so you can care for your baby / Lisa Groen Braner.
    p. cm.
  ISBN 1-57324-822-3
  1. Mothers—Psychology. 2. Mothers—Conduct of life. 3. Motherhood.
  4. Parent and infant. I. Title.
  HQ759 .B273 2003
  306.874'3—dc21   2002010438

Printed in Canada.

03 04 05 06 TCP 10 9 8 7 6 5 4 3 2 1

This book is dedicated to Roger,
for encouraging me to unfurl my wings.

The Mother's Book
of Well-Being

	Prologue	xiii
Introduction	CONCEPTION *Developing the Self*	1
Week 1	DELIVERY *Becoming a Mother*	3
Week 2	THE THROES OF MOTHERHOOD *Keeping Your Sanity*	7
Week 3	SOLITUDE *Finding Time Alone*	11
Week 4	FATHERS *Claiming a Place at the Table*	14

Week 5 WHILE THE WORLD SLEEPS   18
Surviving Sleep Deprivation and Doubts

Week 6 STAYING HOME   22
Defining Work

Week 7 BLISS   26
Uncovering the Holy in the Everyday

Week 8 BODY CONSCIOUSNESS   29
Tuning Into Our Biological Wisdom

Week 9 ROMANCE   32
Making Room for Each Other

Week 10 HOME AGAIN   36
Tending the Hearth

Week 11 MY CLOSET, MY SELF   39
Salvaging the Basics

Week 12 MEASURING MOTHERHOOD   42
Listening to Our Hearts

Week 13 HOME AWAY FROM HOME   45
Casting a Spiritual Net

Week 14 A DAY IN THE LIFE   48
Finding Comfort in a Changing Landscape

Week 15 COUNTING BLESSINGS   51
Summoning a Sense of Gratitude

Week 16 IRREPLACEABLE   54
          Sensing the World Through Baby's Eyes

Week 17 FRAGILE CREATIVITY   57
          Listening and Responding to the Call

Week 18 DEVOTION   60
          Forging a Solitary Path

Week 19 EMPTY MIND   63
          Claiming a Few Moments of Peace

Week 20 MUSIC   67
          Calling Upon a Muse

Week 21 LITERARY ESCAPE   70
          Traveling the World in an Afternoon

Week 22 MOTHER'S DAY   73
          Celebrating It for the First Time

Week 23 WORK IS NO LUXURY   77
          You Don't Need a Job to Take a Break

Week 24 WHO ARE YOU?   80
          Letting Go of the Need to Compare

Week 25 BREAKING DOWN   83
          Reaching Out to a Mother in Need

Week 26 A SETTLING EXPERIENCE   87
          Recognizing the Distance You've Traveled

Week 27 IT'S THE SMALL THINGS   90
         Packing More Than Just Formula

Week 28 VACATION   93
         Swimming into Summer

Week 29 WHAT ABOUT ME?   96
         Widening Our Focus

Week 30 INNOCENCE   99
         Living Our First Life

Week 31 BECOMING FREE   102
         Surrendering the Ego

Week 32 PROGRESS   105
         Longing for the Kitchen

Week 33 BEDTIME   108
         Turning In

Week 34 FAIRY-TALE FAMILIES   112
         Refining the Dream

Week 35 MOMENTS OF FRUSTRATION   115
         Cleaning Up and Moving On

Week 36 IN SEARCH OF REJUVENATION   118
         Taking the Day Off

Week 37 UNLOCKED MEMORIES   121
         Revisiting Your Childhood

Week 38   SOLITUDE REVISITED   124
            Claiming It for Yourself

Week 39   HOME   127
            Calling Us to Ease

Week 40   INVESTMENT OF LOVE   130
            Living in a Troubled World

Week 41   SUPPORTIVE WORDS   133
            Longing for Encouragement

Week 42   WORKAHOLISM   136
            Finding a Balance

Week 43   A MOTHER'S PLAY   140
            Enjoying It

Week 44   WALK WITH THE WIND   143
            Daydreaming and Nostalgia

Week 45   THE DESERT   146
            Creating an Oasis

Week 46   MONEY   149
            Using It Wisely

Week 47   THE LURE OF EFFICIENCY   153
            *Succumbing to the Temptation
            of Tupperware*

Week 48   AUTHENTICITY   156
            Living Your Own Truth

Week 49   HOLIDAYS ANEW   159
            Living in the Moment

Week 50   A SENSE OF PLACE   162
            Driving with Family

Week 51   A BONNET
            Preserving Small Treasures   165

Week 52   A NEW DAY
            Loving Your Child and Yourself 168

            Resource Guide   173

            Acknowledgments   179

            About the Author   181

PROLOGUE

OCCASIONALLY I SEE a new mother out for a walk, pushing a stroller in the middle of the day. Her appearance gives her away. She is disheveled and somehow placid. The frenzied world rushes around without her. Cars race by, their occupants running errands, driving to work, and tending to afternoon routines. My thoughts slow down for a moment and walk with her, remembering all of the changes the first year brings. I recall my uncertainty about motherhood, the changes to my body, my sense of self, and my marriage. I know that these changes are still hazy to her because she's not functioning fully yet. She's recovering from childbirth, surviving on less sleep, and learning to meet the needs of her child.

I notice her attentiveness, and I remember showering my baby with seemingly endless love and affection. She thinks solely about the baby and, probably for the first time in her life, not about herself. Each day renders an elation of experiences—a tiny yawn and snuggle, the curling of little toes, heaven-scented skin. The instinct to stay home is palpable, to retreat to the spotted sunlight of a nursery. A baby's world is focused and small, and a new mother tries to make it loving, nurturing , and satisfying. It's natural to want to give everything she has. So she gives and gives and gives and gives and gives.

Before long, life outside of the nursery door knocks. Phone messages pile up like laundry. The refrigerator and pantry are empty. The house requires cleaning, and the checking account needs to be balanced. Duties mount, and the baby still needs to be held, fed, walked, burped, and rocked. It has been weeks since she has read a newspaper, seen a movie, or gone to dinner with her husband. The work doesn't dwindle, and her child doesn't wait.

As most mothers learn sooner or later, perpetual giving eventually leaves you depleted. Recovering a sense of balance often feels impossible after the tumult of giving birth, breastfeeding, and late nights. Yet it's important that we replenish the well from which we regularly dispense unconditional love. Sometimes we need to escape, have lunch with a friend, or walk in the woods with our mate. We need to make time for our spouse and our friends, who give us the support and strength to care for our children as we do. We also need to take time for our own rest and reflection.

Separating from and returning to our children allow us to see the best in our families and ourselves. Although it seems counterintuitive to most women to think about themselves at this time, it is essential to a balanced and happy home life. That's where this book picks up—at the point when you can't possibly go one more moment without sleep, without a shower, without a smidgen of the life you once lived. This is a time of celebration, and also one of healing and learning. When you gave birth to your baby, you also gave birth to yourself as a mother. You're responsible for another soul and, unexpectedly, newly responsible for yourself.

The passage from woman to mother is complex. It causes us to reexamine who we are and who we want to be for our children. The "guard" of generations has changed. Becoming a mother suddenly places you in the seat of true adulthood. My feet dangle from that chair often. I hasten to touch the ground and sit up straight in my newfound responsibility. Motherhood is a role in which it takes time to become comfortable and confident. The changes are great and the expectations high. We live in a culture that reveres and elevates motherhood to a superhuman stature. So often we come to the role with perceptions of how it will be, and realize how unprepared we really are. All of the plans you made for yourself and your baby before you gave birth may be hard to take during this time of recovery. This may be the first time you've ever been "called" to devote yourself to a job so unconditionally. Some moments will find you strong and tireless, and others will find you exhausted and unsure.

Be gentle with yourself. You are not alone.

There is a mythical path that we walk in becoming mothers, a heroine's journey. When we step into the dark woods, the abyss of the unknown, we come face to face with ourselves—our strengths and our limitations. Our primary work as mothers is to slay the dragons of our psyches that deter us from becoming our most loving Self. We must turn away from those inclinations to deny, burden, and sabotage ourselves. As we learn to care more deeply for ourselves, we extend ourselves more intently to our children. Generosity with one's self begets generosity with one's child. Love begets love. Motherhood is a journey into wholeness, and the way is self-care.

I have been blessed as a mother with two children. Matthew was born first, and his sister Sophia was born two and a half years later. By nature, I am what my husband calls "a planner." I drafted delivery plans for my doctor and nurses, precise birthing strategies emphasized and underlined. My pregnancy books suggested this tactic, and I understand now why my obstetrician placated me by smiling sweetly and sliding them into my file. As it turns out, neither of my deliveries met my careful planning and expectation. And, by the way, neither has motherhood.

Somewhere in the first year, I realized that I was mentally hauling around a "motherhood plan." It took the shape of a simple fantasy—that I would become a perfect mother. It seems improbable to me now that I actually believed this, and if you had asked me if it were true, I would have denied it. Turning to my growing library of how-to-parent texts didn't always help me. Sometimes they reinforced my desire to be more than I was. I longed for a book that would lead me to uncover my own maternal wisdom, comforting words that would soften my self-judgment and smooth my uncertainty. I longed for a book that would speak to my soul. That longing was the genesis of *The Mother's Book of Well-Being*. This book began in the journals that accompanied me through the first years of my children's lives. I showed up at those blank pages often, waiting and watching as a wiser voice scribbled reassuring sentences. I drafted these essays first for myself, and now I share them with you.

Why should we examine our expectations about motherhood? There is a threshold that we cross literally and culturally in becoming a mother, and defining our role is a mixture of accepting and challenging those expectations. This doesn't happen in the first days or weeks of motherhood. The first year is just a good place to start. When we relinquish our tightly held fantasies, we discover a life rich with love, work, and hard-earned satisfaction. We rediscover our true selves. Motherhood renews us; life becomes flush with possibility and hope.

This book is organized in weekly installments to parallel your baby's development, and lead you like stepping stones through the first year. Following each essay is a short section entitled "A Mother of Your Own Design," which encourages you to delve into your own maternal wisdom. You might prefer to read consecutively one essay per week, or turn through them to find one that suits you at any given moment.

As a mother, I share parenting responsibilities with my husband. Although I write about motherhood from the perspective of a partnership, the same tenets of self-care hold true whether you're single or married. Building a supportive community around you is essential to realizing fully your potential as a mother.

I hope that this book can be a guidepost for you, a reminder of the sacred work that fills your days—to become the mother you alone are destined to be. To create, bear, and nurture a new life takes everything a woman possesses, all of her wisdom, intuition, love, and stamina. There is no other job more challenging or fulfilling. Motherhood is a feat that is completely natural and at the same time courageous. Quite possibly, it's the most daunting task we'll ever face. It's also one of the most meaningful.

Lisa Groen Braner

CONCEPTION

Developing the Self

MOTHERHOOD BEGINS at the moment of conception. In that moment, everything shifts.
Life makes way for life. As a woman's belly swells, a slow
but steady understanding dawns. Her maiden time on this
Earth has past. A more mysterious time beckons. She
endures queasy mornings, rife with uncertainty. And as
her baby grows, she begins to understand the meaning of
giving herself over to a child. Her body houses two souls.
Her life is flooded with a sense of wonder and purpose.

During this time of inward change and sacred recognition, a woman's outer world changes also. The identifying
phrase "with baby" says it all. While pregnant, I felt as if
a veil shrouded my physical self, and the only part of me

that people recognized was my abdomen, the baby. I had never felt unseen before pregnancy. Suddenly I was merely a "mother-to-be." This external label affirmed yet contradicted who I was. I was thrilled to become a mother, yet perplexed about losing my own identity. While my identity seemed to narrow to others, it amplified to me.

Being pregnant was my first introduction to the realm of expectation that surrounds motherhood. If I were to write a résumé of the world's perfect mother, it might read like this: responsible, giving, selfless, sacrificing, tireless, strong, moral, wise, kind, forgiving, nurturing, supportive, and so on. No one said it would be easy, but I'm not sure that I want to become someone else's version of the perfect mother. I'd also like to be free-spirited, adventurous, artistic, funny, sensual, and romantic. Rather than blurring one's true self, motherhood can magnify and honor all aspects of who you are. I am a more sensitive writer, a better listener for my friends, a more caring lover.

The first year of motherhood is a time of great change and insight. You will be tested physically, emotionally, intellectually, and spiritually. You'll be pulled to notice the ways in which you care for and neglect yourself. As we walk through these weeks together, I'd like you to open your heart and continue to ask yourself one important question:

What if I were a mother of my own design?

DELIVERY

Becoming a Mother

IN THE BEGINNING, there is light. Perhaps it is only a bright lamp in an otherwise dim delivery room. And then a baby is born. There, in the simple environment of a hospital, a mother is also born. Miracle and mystery conspire in those early moments, despite our ordinary surroundings. We merely show up, and Divinity works through us. We give ourselves over like the Earth does to the seasons, accepting what is inevitable, the simple rotation of a planet around the sun. One's desire for control falls aside in such a moment, and briefly we see how futile our attempts are at directing something so precious. Our babies come to us the way that they do, through pain or elation, and land in our arms for the real adventure.

There is probably no more defining time in a woman's life than walking through the doors of a hospital as one person and walking out two days later as another. I remember thinking this while walking from the parking lot into the maternity center in labor and anticipation. As I stepped through the doors of the maternity ward, I entered a hallowed space. That corridor, with its white walls and gray carpets, felt like a hallway between heaven and earth. My husband and I would meet our baby for the first time in a matter of hours. Would I remain that inspired as bigger waves of labor crashed through me?

As it turns out, I did not feel the slightest bit inspired during my eighteenth hour of labor. I expected it to be difficult, but I also believed I would rise above it somehow and appreciate what was happening. The physical exertion and exhaustion taxed me completely. I sometimes feel guilty that gratitude eluded me in the hours prior to my children's births.

In Louise Erdrich's book *The Blue Jay's Dance,* she asks a question to which I have no answer, "Why is no woman's labor as famous as the death of Socrates? Over all the millennia that women have endured and suffered and died during childbirth, we have no one story that comes down to us with attendant reverence, or that exists in pictures—a cultural icon, like that of Socrates holding forth to his companions as he raises the cup of hemlock." It doesn't surprise me that Erdrich likens giving birth to a self-imposed death. There is a death of sorts, a way of life that ends as another begins. But unlike the story of Socrates, the cultural reverence begins after labor and birth—upon the spirit's entry into a new world. Iconic mothers and maternal symbolism swirl in the mind's eye like leaves in the wind. Idealized images of maternal love and sacrifice fill my consciousness. In the days before birth, we've already begun constructing the nest, plumping and softening it with our hopes and dreams. When my son and daughter finally found their way into our nest, my heart opened up, and they crawled right in.

My dream of an enlightened delivery eluded me. Labor really *is* laborious, and despite all of my effort, one image remains with me—my husband and I waiting on the will of heaven. At the heart of motherhood is the same mystery that encircles us at birth. Spirit is at the center, guiding us with higher wisdom if we choose to listen. It won't always be what we imagine. Despite the hard work, it is often abundantly more.

A Mother of
Your Own Design

- Recognize and appreciate your accomplishment in giving birth. Carrying a child in your body for nine months and then delivering him into the world is some of the most esteemed work you'll ever accomplish. You deserve your own praise now more than ever before. Cherish yourself.

- For nine months, we plan and dream about how our labor and delivery will be. It's not uncommon to feel let down once it's over. I was shocked at how physically difficult it was for me. I wanted to  be with my husband and my baby, but I also wanted to sleep. It's okay to take care of yourself now; in fact it's essential. Make your recovery a priority.

The *Throes* of *Motherhood*

Keeping Your Sanity

Now you are in the throes of motherhood. It didn't take long for life to transform completely. If it feels chaotic and a little shocking, you're in the right place. In the course of one week, you're confronted with hormones, engorgement, and sleeplessness. Your body feels foreign, heavy, and bruised after giving birth. You may be learning to breastfeed, and perhaps houseguests have arrived too.

Adjusting to motherhood is a little like moving to a new town. It will take a while to feel at home here, but be patient. Slowly, you'll become familiar again with your surroundings.

A home nurse visited one week after my first child was born. She carried her scales and stethoscope up our front steps, ready to see if my son and I were healthy. I held my breath when she placed my baby on her scale, hoping that my body was supplying sufficient calories to nourish him. In his first week home, he lost one pound. I was devastated. If only I had achieved a better latch! I scolded myself. I didn't realize that breastfeeding does not always come naturally. In the most essential way of caring for my son, I felt as if I had failed him already. Of course I had not. Many babies lose weight in their first week home. But I cried for a good part of the day, and then I called a lactation consultant.

Lactation consultants, physicians, massage therapists, psychologists, chiropractors, pediatricians, and acupuncturists are professionals who can assist you now. Don't hesitate to contact them for help. Get referrals from friends, doctors, nurses from the maternity ward, and from other mothers. These are tender days for a new mother, so much to do, heal, and learn. Build a community of people around you whom you trust—professionals, family, and friends. You need their support now, and will continue to lean on them in the months ahead.

Whether you're having trouble nursing, or just not feeling good when you get up in the morning, these are days of growing. No one enters into parenting with an advanced degree. We learn through trying, failing, and trying again. It sounds simple but requires persistence and courage.

While gazing at our newborn babies, snuggled still and sleeping, it's natural to want to be perfect for them. But *perfect* isn't an adjective that even the most experienced mother would use to describe herself. Let's stop evaluating ourselves by our first attempts, and focus instead on how we are evolving. Let's consider our good intentions. Let's care for ourselves as we would our children, unconditionally.

A Mother of *Your Own Design*

- The first weeks of motherhood are often the most challenging. While you're adjusting, family and friends will swoop into your home to offer their help. It's natural for them to want to celebrate your baby's arrival and help in this transition. Don't feel the need to play hostess. Relax and appreciate this opportunity to recuperate. Let them clean and cook for you. Ask them to organize the baby's drawers or closet. Houseguests can assist you with announcements and thank-you notes. This is a time to rest and enjoy your baby.

- Remember these early days by beginning a
  motherhood journal. Use a tape recorder or a
  pen—whichever is easiest. Record the highs and
  lows. Record the amazing and the mundane.
  Take a few minutes whenever the urge moves you,
  not necessarily every day, and remember
  your feelings about this time.

*S*OLITUDE

Finding Time Alone

T HESE EARLY DAYS OF motherhood are all-consuming. Even if you have older children, a new baby introduces you to a completely new way of life. Just remembering to eat lunch is difficult. When a friend's son was two weeks old, she asked her husband to come home from work so that she could brush her teeth and comb her hair. Before I had a child, I thought she was exaggerating. Now I know how precious a few minutes of solitude are during the day. Gone are uninterrupted spaces for quiet contemplation. A mother's time and thoughts are no longer just her own once a baby arrives; yet the urge to commune with one's thoughts and experiences does not go away.

Jennifer Louden, author of *The Woman's Comfort Book*, says, "Solitude is an essential self-nurturing activity. It helps us avoid fragmentation and burnout and encourages us to rebuild ourselves, to process our experiences." Seeking solitude in the earliest weeks of motherhood often seems impossible, particularly when you are the primary caregiver. We become so used to meeting our children's needs, responding to their every discomfort, that we feel personally accountable for their every breath. This sense of duty is exhausting and, well, unrealistic.

When it seems impossible to break away from responsibilities, that's usually the time to escape for a while. We often don't listen to ourselves until it's too late—until we snap at loved ones, or worse, become sick. If we don't give ourselves that time, we can't care as well for others. Taking time for solitude is not a luxury; it's essential to everyone's happiness.

New babies both bless and wreak havoc on a home. Adjusting to the busyness of everyday life can be jarring. Now is the time to create habits that nurture you as a mother. When you nurture yourself, you will nurture your family. When you value and respect yourself, your children will grow to value and respect you. When you step outside of your everyday routine to find peace within yourself, you will create a peaceful home.

Babies tune our hearing outward. We distinguish between cries of hunger and cries of fatigue. We listen for them while we're awake and asleep. Having a baby pulls us outside of ourselves by necessity. But let's not forget to keep an ear open to the cry of our inner voice too. Finding time for solitude encourages us to listen to ourselves. In those quiet moments alone, ask yourself what you need to feel nourished. Honor the answers that come. As mothers, we meet our children's needs a hundred times a day. Let us remember to ask ourselves what we need to feel nurtured at least once a day.

A Mother of
Your Own Design

- Carve out time today to pull a few weeds from your garden, watch the clouds from your backyard, or enjoy a cup of tea by candlelight. Try to spend at least 30 minutes listening to your own voice, stepping away from the noise and work around you.

- Make a list of activities and things that you love or crave. Include simple pleasures as well as extravagant ones. Your list might include regular massages, and it also might include watching sunsets from your backyard. Don't think too much about it; just go with your instincts. Post your list somewhere visible.

FATHERS

Claiming a Place at the Table

T HE BABY CRIES, the bottles boil, and the crib needs new sheets. Where is your partner? Let's hope seeing to one or more of the above. We rush around as mothers, preparing, answering, and planning. We immediately take the helm, instinctively pouring ourselves into the job like formula into bottles. Perhaps our partners defer when we dash about the house, crazed with hormones and good intentions. It's easier to do it ourselves, we might reason, or perhaps we don't even notice. But fathers have good intentions too.

This is a time when roles are being defined. What does it mean to be a mother in your home? You've probably thought about this more than you realize. Every impulse to nurture, clean, and smooth is a reflection of your feelings about motherhood. What, then, are your feelings on fatherhood? I want my children to have an involved and nurturing father, one who cradles them when they're sick and jostles them when they're well.

Women have more time to get used to the idea of parenting than men do. Carrying a baby for nine months teaches us to move over for the life to come. Pregnancy conditions our thinking by necessity. Our role changes as soon as our bodies do, but for fathers, birth is the beginning. Mothers react like runners at a starting line, conditioned athletes who've prepared mentally for months before the race. At the sound of the gun, fathers are often just arriving at the stadium.

For the first week after my son was born, my husband spent hours in a woodshop finishing a dresser that he designed from scratch. It is beautiful, natural ash wood with pewter starfish handles. I loved his dedication to it when I was pregnant, but after the baby was born, I couldn't understand why he would leave for hours to work on it instead of staying home with us. Now I know. His carpentry was an expression of his love; he felt useless at home. At least he could busy himself in the shop. He believed that I knew what I was doing.

As it turns out, nine months of mental preparation is no match for experience. I knew as little about caring for our baby as he did. Once I convinced him that I needed him home more than our son needed his dresser, we began to learn together.

Parenting at its best is a partnership. Mothers and fathers may bring different qualities, but no one gender trumps the other in natural expertise. In the first year, and particularly these first months, bonds are forged. Babies form bonds with their parents, but perhaps the most important bond is that between father and mother. A supportive and shared dedication to our children gives them the best of both worlds. Two nurturing hearts are better than one, and four helping hands are always better than two.

A Mother of
Your Own Design

+ Caring for a baby can seem to fall naturally into a mother's lap, especially if you're breastfeeding. But fathers can bathe, clothe, rock, change, and sing to babies. If you're a single mother, accept offers of support from family members and friends. Try to share as much of the responsibility as possible, and try not to be critical.

- Allow your partner an opportunity to spend time with the baby alone. Take an hour or two to buy some comfortable clothing, a necessity while you're breastfeeding and still losing weight. Or if you prefer, find a good book at the library and settle into an empty couch for a couple of chapters.

WHILE THE WORLD SLEEPS

Surviving Sleep Deprivation and Doubts

IT'S EASY TO REMEMBER how thankful you are to be a mother when your baby's smiling and content. It's much harder, if not impossible, said my friend Lydia, when it's three o'clock in the morning and she hasn't slept for longer than 45 minutes at a stretch. Her honesty traveled over the phone lines separating us and eased my guilty conscience. I couldn't remember how long it had been since I had slept for four hours straight, let alone an entire night. I had recently crossed over from ungrateful to plain resentful when rolling out of bed in the wee hours of the morning. If sleeplessness weren't enough torment, inner questions of character and strength beseeched me. How can I resent a small child who is only crying out for comfort? What is wrong with me?

Christina Baker Kline writes about a mother's life after midnight in her book *Child of Mine*: "Standing at the window, I look across the street at the rows of apartment windows and imagine another sleepless mother holding a baby in a dimly lit room. How many of us are there, I wonder, each in her own home, perhaps far from family, without ready access to other mothers who might provide a sense of community?"

I often think about mothers who are rocking their babies in the dark. I wish to talk with them, share my frustrations and lean on them for strength. I miss my mother, sisters, aunts, and grandmothers. Far away from my family, I feel the miles stretch long between us.

One of the strangest aspects of motherhood is the loneliness one feels despite the fact that so many other women assume the same journey. Even if a woman has strong support from friends and family, motherhood tends to be a solitary endeavor. No one can replace her, even temporarily. This task before us, to rear a human being, is a staggering responsibility. How could we possibly avoid moments of ambivalence, desperation, and uncertainty?

There is a mythological mother to whom I often compare myself. She is well rested, all knowing, infinitely patient and nurturing. She embodies all of my maternal ideals, and although I try, I can't seem to live up to her example. Of course, she's not real. But that doesn't seem to stop me from trying to become her. Sometimes I see glimpses of her in other mothers I know. My friend Michelle's home is so peaceful, and I see the same peace reflected in her children. Genevieve sits captivated while listening to her young children, honoring their ideas and bolstering their individuality. Denise throws her arms around her sons, and I see comfort cross each of their faces, content with her affection. Ellis speaks to her kids respectfully, and they in turn act more respectfully. My friends show me glimpses of the Divine in spite of their humanity, and I feel hopeful. I hope that my own child will come to see qualities in me that outshine my obvious weaknesses and limitations.

In those blurry morning hours, I try to remember that my feelings are only temporary. When I forgive and trust myself at my most challenging moments, the best I have to give always resurfaces. As faithfully as dawn graces the world outside of my bedroom window, maternal love rises in my heart again and again.

A Mother of
Your Own Design

- Maintain your relationships with family and friends. Mothers often feel isolated and lonely during a child's first year. Motherhood brings many joys and challenges. It is perfectly normal to feel overwhelmed by all of the changes happening in

your life. Mothers' support groups,
including those found on the
Internet, can be of great help
during this time.

- Sleep deprivation is a way of life for
  most new families in a baby's first year. You've
  heard the advice from many: Sleep while the baby
  sleeps. Although it's tempting to use a baby's
  naptime to do other things around the house, try
  to devote some or all of the time to your own rest.
  Sleep is as precious to your body as water. Don't
  neglect it. Take turns with your partner getting up
  during the night. Parenting in the first year requires
  physical stamina, and your health requires as much
  attention and sleep as you can give it.

STAYING HOME

Defining Work

"DO YOU WORK?" someone asks innocently for the first time since you've had your baby. When you're mastering the full-time logistics of caring for an infant, and feeling good about it, this question can stop you in your tracks. "Well," I've always wanted to answer, "I'm on call 24 hours a day, rarely get a break longer than 15 minutes, and my muscles are constantly fatigued from heavy lifting." Work is hovering over your child's crib for hours when she's sick with her first cold. Work is getting up four times a night to feed a newborn baby. Work is singing to a crying baby while doing the laundry and attempting to eat a few bites of cereal.

The question itself says so much about how we value mothers, whether or not our contributions matter. But the interesting part of that question lies in one's inability to answer it satisfactorily—because no matter how you answer, it may not be good enough for whoever is asking the question. If we do work outside of the home, are we involved enough with our children? If we don't work outside of the home, do we still have the capacity to think? We revere mothers for not putting their children in daycare and condemn those who "lose it" while staying home with their kids. Mothers themselves feel guilty about the choice to pursue a life outside of parenting. "Shouldn't I feel more inclined to be with him all of the time? What kind of mother am I?" We torment ourselves, questioning our character as if motherhood requires more than we are.

It doesn't.

That's right, we are enough. What's more, we are enough exactly as we are. Why is this a revelation? All our lives, we're taught to just be ourselves and we'll find our way. Yet when it comes to motherhood, we often try to squeeze into shoes that are much too small. We buy into the concept of maternal sacrifice early, placing ourselves secondary to our children. It's an easy change to make, because after all, a helpless infant's needs *should* come first. Isn't this the line that runs through our heads all day and all night?

Caring for a baby has a tendency to drown out everything else—your needs, your marriage, and especially your interests. If we can bring ourselves back into the front seat of our lives, we might become more generous and content caregivers. We get into trouble as mothers when we neglect the essence of who we are. Our children do not need a nameless faceless mother; they need a unique and passionate caregiver who loves her life. We cannot live for someone else. Becoming a mother is a choice. We choose to devote our time and energy to our children, living our own lives in the process.

Balancing the needs of a baby with our own needs is not always simple. We teeter one way or the other, usually away from ourselves. The key is to remain aware of how we feel along the way. When we honor the whole of ourselves, external opinions don't affect us. We don't feel the need to fit into someone else's ideals. We need merely to listen to ourselves and lead the way.

A Mother of *Your Own Design*

• In your motherhood journal, list the ways having a baby has changed your life. (Yes, this will be a long list. Don't leave anything out.) What parts of yourself have you left behind?

- Design an ideal day for yourself. If you're an artist, it might include painting in the evenings. An ideal day also might include a leisurely breakfast and a good night's sleep. Usually the things we crave are within our reach; we simply need to be more creative about attaining them now.

Week 7

Bliss

Uncovering the Holy in the Everyday

A moment can sear into one's memory forever, instantly recalled by a scent, a season, or even a shadow cast by the afternoon sun. One of the earliest memories I have of motherhood is sitting beside a picture window on the sofa with my son—then only a few weeks old—his body warm against mine, soundly sleeping. Pink azaleas bloomed beyond the glass, against a lawn just sprouting in the early spring. It was a moment draped in bliss.

Motherhood can do that for you. The day careens wildly from one duty to the next until suddenly, gratefully, it pauses for a moment of sacred recognition. If you listen, you can hear two hearts beating. Mothers usher new life into the world. We dabble in the sacred daily, amidst the laundry and the diapers. Who knew such treasure would be found within the curve of one's own arm? This life we lead is exceptional, measured by moments instead of hours, love instead of advantage.

Our devotion allows us to step beyond ourselves and in the process leads us more deeply into the truth of who we are. We are full of love, hope, and grace. Even God seems more accessible; we've become partners in work of a higher dimension. Like a miracle, exhaustion and uncertainty can evaporate instantly with a few seconds of wonder. Eyelashes flutter sleepily, brushing against my shoulder. There is no place my son would rather be. His comfort spills onto me, trickling peace like water over a stone. I think to myself that this is somehow reversed, that I am the one who usually gives him comfort. And I do, in the ways of this Earth. He, on the other hand, brings me back to a place free of time and pressure. He brings me back to the soulful joys of nature, sleep, and cherishing someone you love.

Our children have something to teach us. They lead us beyond the realm of the everyday. We work hard, and unexpectedly the seemingly mundane turns holy. I find myself wondering how long the azaleas have been blooming. Why didn't I notice them before now? No matter, this moment is full enough. And as if in agreement, my son sighs and nestles more deeply into my arms.

A Mother of
Your Own Design

- Keep an eye out this week for transcendent moments lurking beneath laundry and late nights. They're instantly recognizable. When you find yourself in a moment draped in bliss, pause. Enjoy the blessings in your life.

- How can you become more available to these blessings? As you go about your day, are you paying attention? Notice the touch of flannel, the warmth of a baby's cheeks, the coo of a newborn, the scent of baby's skin.

BODY CONSCIOUSNESS

Tuning Into Our Biological Wisdom

WITHIN THE COURSE of about one year, your body has physically endured pregnancy, birth, breastfeeding, sleep deprivation, and the demands of carrying a growing baby. Emotionally you've endured the same, in addition to navigating through these uncertain waters of parenting. We're faced with our inexperience, and crawl slowly toward confidence as parents. We're learning as much about ourselves as we are about caring for our children.

These lessons, some of the most intense we'll experience, can take a toll on our physical selves. Once the immediacy of a baby's care wanes, our bodies come sharply back into focus. You might feel a knot above your right shoulder blade that tightens while nursing, or a pain in your lower back that has never really healed from pregnancy. Your knees might ache. All of these symptoms are messages, the body's way of asking for help. We should not endure pain; rather we should find our way to its relief, possibly in the hands of a health practitioner we trust.

"We are all living history books," says Caroline Myss, Ph.D., author of *Anatomy of the Spirit*. "Our bodies contain our histories—every chapter, line, and verse of every event and relationship in our lives. As our lives unfold, our biological health becomes a living, breathing biographical statement." What is your body telling you?

In giving birth to my son, I sprained my coccyx (tailbone) and felt chronic pain while sitting for weeks. My medical doctor told me that I would heal slowly, possibly not for three months or more. I knew that my son would require more physically from me than I had, so my health became a top priority. I turned to holistic practitioners, scheduling appointments with a skilled massage therapist and chiropractor. Thanks to cranial-sacral therapy, spinal manipulation, and light sports massage, my injury improved rapidly. I continue to care for my back through exercise and yoga, and I don't hesitate to schedule more massage or chiropractic work if I need it.

In *Eight Weeks to Optimum Health,* Andrew Weil, M.D., defines health as "wholeness and balance, an inner resilience that allows you to meet the demands of living without being overwhelmed. . . . Optimal health should also bring with it a sense of strength and joy, so that you experience it as more than just the absence of disease."

Chronic pain moved me to consider my health more seriously. Attend to your health before that happens. The human body is a sea of consciousness prone toward healing. It tries to work with us, around our fatigue, in spite of our diet or lack of exercise. Eventually, though, we need to participate, listening to the messages our bodies murmur. Motherhood stretches us physically and emotionally beyond where we've been before. Our health is more important than ever.

A Mother of
Your Own Design

- Take fifteen minutes or so to scan over your body mentally. What do you feel? Have you been neglecting any part of your physical health lately? Why?

- Resolve to participate more actively with your health. You might need to visit a physician, nutritionist, exercise physiologist, or other practitioner. If so, research your healthcare options, and ask for recommendations from friends.

Week 9

ROMANCE
Making Room for Each Other

HOW IS IT POSSIBLE to have time for romance? After childbirth, the word seemed to drop from my vocabulary completely. More primary needs must be met, a decent night's sleep for one. When my first child was born, our home life revolved around him. I remember sitting in the living room learning how to breastfeed, while watching the video *Braveheart* with Mel Gibson. I was distracted, as I'd been for the nine months prior, my attention turned to making room in my life for my son. My son's nursery was the most organized, decorated, and comfortable room in the house. I had read every book about pregnancy and motherhood published, and collected every modern baby convenience available. I lived in a world of perpetual domesticity.

It surprised me when, transfixed by Mel Gibson's physique and blue eyes, I began to melt into the sofa. He called to me, beckoning me into a world where I wasn't a mother anymore. Had Mel stepped out of my television and asked me to run away with him in that instant, I would have said Yes. In my most physically exhausted and unattractive state, I craved romance. My mind had been swathed in pastel flannel for too long.

Caring for children, as satisfying as it is, is not enough for a woman. It's certainly not enough for a marriage, either. Babies have a way of striking romance from your life. The freedom to be alone at will with your partner is gone. Quiet weekend interludes are no longer an option with an infant. It's a side effect of parenting that sneaks up on you when the first thrilling and exhaustive weeks are over. One's need for romance and intimacy doesn't go away, but the opportunities to cultivate it dwindle to near extinction. How then does romance resurface?

By finding simple ways to care for one another amidst the chaos. When my husband lights a candle and draws a bath for me at the end of the night, I remember how much I love him. When I arrange for a babysitter, if only for an hour to go out for dessert and coffee, he appreciates the time I give to him uninterrupted. The need to connect with your spouse is heightened now. Making your partner the focus of your attention, however you're able, is the fastest way to rekindle romance in your life. The more attention and care you give your marriage, the more satisfying it becomes.

It's easy to become tangled in the duties and demands of parenting, but don't deny your marriage in the process. Reawakening a romantic life benefits both your child and your marriage. A strong relationship bolsters your efforts as parents, lending support and strength during the challenging times. It will also give your child a foundation of love upon which he will draw for the rest of his life.

A Mother of
Your Own Design

- Connect and talk with your partner at the beginning and end of every day. Resume some of the hobbies you loved together before you had children. Could the baby watch a tennis game from her stroller on the court? Could you take hikes together with her in a front pack? Could you go to a movie on Saturday night and let her sleep on your shoulder?

- Schedule a date with your partner this week and write it on the calendar. Choose a favorite destination. Ask a family member or friend to watch the baby for you. You may feel nervous about leaving her for the first time, but leave a phone number and walk out the door. Spending time with your partner is now a conscious decision. Your baby will be fine without you for a couple hours.

Week 10

Home Again

Tending the Hearth

Before having a baby, keeping a clean, organized, and comfortable home was optional. Groceries could be purchased every other day, and there was always time to do a last-minute load of laundry. Life seemed to happen outside of the home anyway; it was a mere stopping point between work and play, a return address.

A baby changes all of that, drawing one's attention back to the home. Sharing home with a child, whether a city dwelling or a house in the suburbs, changes its purpose. It becomes a refuge, a place to feed our bodies, nurture our souls, and dream about our futures. We find ourselves caring more about it; it is our shelter and safe haven from the outside. But maintaining a home takes time, and it also takes help.

There is no universal measurement of adequate cleanliness and organization; don't be pressured to think otherwise—by advertisements, friends, family, or our perfectionist culture. Everyone has certain standards that they must maintain to keep sane. I personally can live with dust but not clutter. If your home has not yet recovered from the busyness of babyhood, decide which tasks around the house are essential to your peace of mind, and involve whomever you must to get them done. They don't have to be finished tomorrow. You can make small strides over time—finding a basket for bills that clutter your countertops, organizing a drawer or two in the kitchen while you talk on the phone, or finding a resting place for keys, diaper bags, and shoes left by the front door. Our home reflects how we feel about ourselves. As parents, our home also reflects what we wish to give to our children. Keeping organized and making time for the tasks that keep your home running efficiently creates a peaceful refuge for everyone.

The sight of a filled refrigerator, stacked with leftover vegetable stew and strawberries, can feel more abundant than a brimming bank account. Polishing the wood of an antique table, bringing it back to life with the skill of our hands, becomes a meditation as we smooth it over and over again. Caught by the fragrance of narcissus bulbs on the kitchen windowsill, rinsing dishes in the sink comes close to a prayer.

When a baby enters the home, sunlight bounces through the house more intently, filling the rooms with the golden color of childhood. The outside world becomes distant, almost foreign in the presence of a baby. The simplest pleasures of homemaking return, evoking memories of our own youth. Babies draw us back willingly to the lure and warmth of tending the hearth.

A Mother of
Your Own Design

- We can either fight housework or see it for what it is: an extension of caring for ourselves and our children. It's okay to hire a professional or neighborhood teen if you need help. Start small by noticing where clutter gathers in your home. Place baskets, hooks, or shelves in strategic places.

- How are you most inclined to tend to the hearth? Does it include baking? Skim through cookbooks and choose a recipe for crusty bread or morning muffins. Do you love to garden? Plant an indoor herb garden or force fragrant spring bulbs on a sunny window ledge. Do you enjoy sewing? Visit a fabric store and choose some beautiful fabric to drape a window or dining room table. Whatever the urge, choose an inexpensive project that can be enjoyed and completed in a couple of hours.

My Closet, My Self

Salvaging the Basics

L ET'S FACE IT, having a baby changes your body forever. Gone are my illusions of returning to the smallest jeans hanging in my closet. I've had them since my first year of college, and because of their sentimental value, I can't throw them away. I've managed to fit into them a few times since, but all of that seems so distant now. My mind flashes many memories as I glance at those small jeans—leisurely mornings at my favorite coffeehouse before class, laughing with friends over lunch, midnight romps with an old boyfriend. I rarely ate breakfast, and sleep was usually plentiful. My exercise consisted of walking to class and dancing on the weekends, and that was more than enough. Let's just place all of these pre-baby memories in the "Things I don't do now" category and shut the closet door. But forgive me if I can't seem to part with these old jeans. They're sometimes the only evidence I have of my young childless self.

I know that I'm not alone in this effort to treasure my small jeans. The mothers who exercise with me at my gym probably have them hanging in their closets too. We alternately climb onto the treadmills and scales, trying to find our way back. I know it's not realistic to want my pre-baby body. But I think it's okay to mourn it occasionally.

A friend called me the other day to ask if I knew about laser resurfacing for stretch marks. She was desperate thinking that she may never be able to wear a bikini again. Sound shallow? I have a feeling that her bikini signifies more than mere vanity. Like my small jeans, her bikini may carry memories too—surfing waves off the coast of Hawaii, sunbathing with girlfriends who couldn't keep secrets, hitchhiking with her husband before they were married.

Our bodies serve many purposes in this life, and now their purpose is shifting away from our own exclusive pleasure to bearing, nourishing, and sustaining life for another human being. It's not glamorous or thrilling to give oneself over so completely. In fact, it's pretty difficult at times. This transition from always thinking about myself to rarely thinking about myself has not been easy for me. It's probably not easy for anyone, no matter how ready they are for parenthood. Our bodies are the homes we live in for a lifetime, and having a baby changes our residence completely. It's okay to miss the old, but at some point we also need to embrace the new.

A new pair of jeans hangs in my closet, next to my small ones. They're comfortable, soft, and a little more forgiving. I really do like them, too, and I wonder if one day I'll treasure them as much as I have treasured my small jeans. Will they carry memories of my son climbing into my lap on a stormy afternoon? Or eating watermelon with my daughter on the front lawn, her face and fingers sticky and pink? I have a feeling that they might.

A Mother of
Your Own Design

- Find the "small jeans" in your closet (or any item of clothing from the past that you cherish). Hold them in your hands and reminisce about who you were before the baby was born, and perhaps before you were married.

- Choose one favorite activity from that time in your life and plan a date this week to do it, by yourself, with your spouse or friends, but without the baby. Find time, find child care, and enjoy yourself.

Week 12

Measuring Motherhood

Listening to Our Hearts

T HERE IS SOME comfort in calendars and clocks, the way the days and minutes march predictably by like soldiers in uniform. I've leaned on them during uncertain times, relying upon the promise of a new hour, day, or week. Life is somehow simpler when it's sliced into edible morsels. Before motherhood, daily schedules kept me going, pushed me onward. Tasks would be finished and a new schedule of tasks would begin. I knew where I was going and where I had been. I needed only to turn back a few pages, or glance at the clock to remember.

Motherhood shifts us away from all of that—the measurable ease of crossing through lists and counting time. Our work diverges from day planners and crosses a bridge from efficiency to sufficiency. We are sufficient as mothers when we show up, open to whatever the day brings. But being particularly addicted to lists, I have not given up on them altogether. My maternal "To do" list resembles a journal entry more than a day planner. I list the mundane tasks that I face daily and the intangible items as well, especially all the virtues in which I'm deficient. And somehow, these never seem to get crossed off my list. How does one quantify progress in patience, for example?

Oh, there are times when it's tempting to simplify this complex work of rearing children to something measurable, but parenting is more elusive than that. I have sat in my neighbor's house, gazing at her perpetually vacuumed carpets, and believed for an instant that she personifies all of the virtues that a mother should possess. Surely if she provides floors on which her children could eat and sleep, she has mastered this role. Clean floors are much easier to attain than patience, and I'm ready to feel good about having them even if I'm deluding myself temporarily.

In truth, motherhood is largely invisible. It requires more than vacuuming. We can't evaluate our performance by counting how many times we've changed a diaper or wiped a nose. Our work includes those things, but it's fueled by a richer motivation to nurture, guide, and love. A good day might include a clean home, but it always involves connecting with our children. On those days I feel full, satiated by the work of caring and giving. I fall into bed with a gratifying fatigue that comes only after putting in a good day's work. When my daughter smiled after rolling over for the first time, I knew my work was simply to witness her pride. When my son marvels at the crunch of autumn under his feet, I know that there's nothing more important than our walk in the woods. These activities are impossible to pin down to a date on the calendar. I'm not sure that I'd want my life to be that predictable anyway. Becoming a mother requires you to throw away the desire to plan and control. The sweetest aspects of motherhood are the immeasurable ones—gauged only by one's heart.

A Mother of
Your Own Design

• Which qualities do you envy or admire in other mothers? Separate their invisible qualities from the visible. Which are more important to you?

• When you doubt yourself as a mother, let go of the productivity of your day. Focus on connecting with your child instead. Have a picnic of baby snacks and milk. Roll around in the grass and watch clouds. Light candles after dark and tell stories. Notice how you feel.

Home Away from Home

Casting a Spiritual Net

THERE IS A PLACE where I reside for only one hour every week, yet within that hour, all of my cares subside. They're lifted up and carried away by voices joined in song. Comforting phrases pass my lips, and the air around me feels softer than usual. Sunlight filters through jewel-tone colored glass, and strangers willingly scoot over in their seats to make room for latecomers. My reverence and hope magnify each Sunday morning as I gather with others, sharing hymns, prayers, and silence. Within the walls of this sanctuary I understand the salutation, "God's peace." It settles within me during the hour, shifting my feelings and thoughts away from whatever consumed me before I entered. I leave another person, more forgiving and content.

My spiritual life did not always include the ritual of attending church. My sense of wonder and connection with the universe ebbed and flowed, relying less upon ritual and more upon happenstance. For me, having children has pushed me to claim one morning a week that is devoted to prayer. I need to walk into the doors of that sanctuary like a garden needs water in the summer sun.

Motherhood is a sacred path, inviting a new soul to share in one's life. We can enter into it consciously, cultivating a sense of gratitude and strength. Each of us has a relationship with God that is unique, a fingerprint in the cosmos, but sometimes we have to cast our spiritual net to gather gifts from heaven. Attending church is one way. Meditation, prayer, and solitude also connect us to a wiser part of ourselves. The rituals we choose should hold personal meaning, compelling us to practice and remember. Morrie Schwartz, the late Brandeis University professor whose life lessons were recorded in *Tuesdays with Morrie,* told his students, "Find what is divine, holy or sacred for you. Attend to it, or worship it in your own way."

Choosing a spiritual path is not like shopping for food, when any grocery store will suffice. It requires an excavation of the self and an expedition of sorts. You might feel inclined to dip yourself into different religious communities, listening and watching. Or perhaps you'll revisit the religion of your youth. You might find your sanctuary in a yoga class or a meditation center. Eventually you'll find a place that appeals to you, and when that happens, you'll recognize it at once. Finding your path is like meeting a new friend, someone you feel you've known forever.

Church is a ritual that nurtures my spirit. Readings and sermons occasionally drift past me, but there is a life force underneath the words that sustains me. I reconnect with myself, and as a result, I walk back into my life and reconnect more passionately with my loved ones.

A Mother of
Your Own Design

- Do you have a spiritual practice? If you're searching for ways to connect to Spirit, what are you looking for? God? Peace? Fellowship? Guidance? What is your spiritual background? Where do you feel most comfortable? Using these answers, choose three spiritual practices or religious institutions and attend their services in the next month.

- When choosing rituals, consistency is key. Choose rituals that you look forward to, that connect you to a reality larger than yourself.

Week 14

A Day in the Life

Finding Comfort in a Changing Landscape

T HE DECISION TO STAY at home with a baby is sometimes an easier decision to make than it is to live. Priorities shift, labor shifts, and life becomes defined by the needs and happiness of one's child. It's difficult to admit sometimes how challenging that choice can be. Our culture usually paints motherhood as a time of joy, fulfillment, and unspeakable happiness. But let's sit comfortably with the whole truth. As wonderful as it is at times, this job of mothering is hard work.

It's Monday morning and the clock strikes six. Before having a child, you might have been rising to get the newspaper and a lingering cup of coffee. You might have been thinking about the details of your workday, and after a hot shower and a quiet drive to work, you'd sink your whole self into your job.

With children our days defy the clock; hours and minutes stretch or shrink depending on the task at hand. Six o'clock in the morning means nothing when you've been wakened throughout the night. A 15-minute inconsolable crying jag in the grocery store feels like a day's worth of work. Bathing and feeding, some of the most endearing moments, drift easily and fully. When a baby is sleeping, snug and peaceful in her nursery, two hours fly by like the tapping of fingernails on a desk. When the baby spits up on you for the fourth time in an hour, you gaze at the clock, certain that the day is almost over, and it is only 2:30.

We have a human tendency to want to speed up our lives to what's enjoyable. We look to the future or remember the past to avoid what is right here, now. It doesn't help if we compare our own experience to the cultural legend of motherhood. When we deny what is, we may miss the sudden sweetness of a baby lying on our chest, breathing softly on our neck. And if our children were always at peace, we may not recognize the sacred power of easing their worry by touch. Let's look at motherhood as a landscape rather than a single garden—a landscape rich with steep mountains and rolling valleys. A landscape is beautiful in its entirety, as the composite of motherhood can be as well.

Motherhood is an intricate undertaking full of challenges and revelations. When we feel most vulnerable, at the mercy of our own limitations, we discover ourselves anew. We are stronger and more resourceful than we could have imagined. Our work is unlike any other; it's more about discovery than about productivity. It requires our awareness and forgiveness. We don't need to be maternal heroines, immune to the emotional and physical effects of catering all day long to the needs of a baby. What we need is a dose of realism, that this *is* in fact hard work. You're not imagining it. You're doing the best you can.

A Mother of *Your Own Design*

- At the end of your day today, list your top three difficult parenting moments. How did you respond to them? How did your responses surprise you? If you feel unhappy with your reactions, craft a plan to respond differently next time.

- How has motherhood made you more resourceful? Make a list and post it over your baby's changing table.

COUNTING BLESSINGS

Summoning a Sense of Gratitude

AFTER MY KIDS WENT to bed tonight, I turned the corner from the hallway to my living room and caught sight of the remnants of my day—burp cloths draped over every piece of furniture, my children's laundry heaped in a corner waiting to be washed, and the baby swing sitting in the center of the room. Exhausted, I couldn't pick up one more thing. I just sat down and surveyed the chaotic echo of my day. My eyes drifted from one mess to another until slowly, I saw the floor that they lay on. I thought of our roof that covered the mess. I gazed beyond our dirty windows to moonlight stretching across the backyard. I thought of our refrigerator, not the sticky prints on the outside, but the food inside. My daughter's laundry is warm clothing. And my baby swing is pure luxury.

At that moment there were mothers who were worried about feeding their children, sustaining their water supply, protecting them from the weather, or war. I imagined their prayers. There are children in this world who have never known basic shelter, who always know hunger. For their mothers, such need must be a slow torture.

With this in mind, my domestic tasks of laundry, cooking, and corralling clutter transformed. They became daily rituals that I am blessed to perform for my family. How many mothers are there who wish for similar circumstances? Gratitude lifted the mask of my fatigue. I stopped striving for order and cleanliness. I was grateful and content to live my life as it was then—messy and abundant. Finally my children were in bed, and suddenly I found myself cherishing them. Laundry is a small price to pay for a morning of cuddling with a baby. My son's latest rendition of "Old MacDonald," replete with new and improved animal sounds, requires a certain amount of jumping and twirling. He didn't remember he was holding a cup full of Cheerios, which quickly turn to dust when stepped on.

Gratitude comes easily when life flows smoothly, but how do we cultivate it when it tumbles stubbornly into hard-to-reach places, like dust bunnies under beds? To feel grateful for your life, study all that surrounds you. Tune into your senses—see the sunrise while you tie back the curtains in your bedroom, listen to your baby's voice as she endeavors to speak, taste a bowl of ice cream with your husband after the kids are in bed, nestle with your baby during an afternoon nap. Our most treasured memories usually hang on the edge of mere moments—brushing blonde tresses or buttoning blue overalls.

Will I continue to be grateful tomorrow, when my toddler smears his peanut butter-coated fingers on the walls? Or when my three-month-old spits up her milk on my fourth clean shirt of the day? I'm not sure I will. But for now, I know that all of it is okay. In fact, it's idyllic.

A Mother of
Your Own Design

- Our lives as mothers are especially lush and tender, and caring for a young baby is fleeting. Before our eyes, they will grow older, and we will have to learn to share them with the rest of the world. Now is the time to recognize how lovely it is to hold them in our arms.

- A busy and loving home is going to be messy at times. Rather than focusing on the dishes in the sink, try to appreciate the less visible work that occurs in your home daily—the love and care of your child.

Week 16

IRREPLACEABLE

Sensing the World Through Baby's Eyes

You are irreplaceable in your baby's life. Others may influence her, guide her, and love her, but you alone are her mother. A child comes into the world through you and will understand the world largely through you. By the age of four months, she has begun an identification process called "imitation." Through imitation, a baby acts and feels like her mother. Our children, in a sense, make us a part of themselves. They learn who they are through this earliest relationship in life. Are you the person you would like your child to be?

In *Diary of a Baby,* Daniel Stern, M.D., writes about a fictional baby named Joey, who is placed on his mother's lap. While gazing at Joey, a smile lights up the mother's face, and Joey responds. "In reaching across to touch him, her smile exerts its natural evocative powers and sets in motion its contagiousness.... It makes him resonate with the animation she feels and shows. His joy rises." Joey smiles back. This exchange between mother and child is one of the earliest forms of self-identification and socialization. Likewise, when a mother is preoccupied or troubled about something, she also influences her child. Stern writes, "After about three months, when babies know what to expect in a face-to-face encounter with their mother, they get disturbed if she deviates far from the usual. Unable exactly to know her state, [Joey] can capture only the vague and confusing sense of her mentally hovering somewhere else.... In identifying with her, he feels her emotional dullness creeping into himself."

Our children are directly affected by us, and indirectly affected by how well we care for ourselves. When we are healthy, our interactions with them are healthy. When we are troubled—with relationships, work, or otherwise—we are not the only ones who endure it. Becoming a mother causes us to think beyond ourselves, but we cannot forget ourselves in the process. It is not in the best interest of our children to deny our own needs. The act of self-nurturing is not selfish; it's essential to us and to the health of our families. The first months of motherhood can be the most physically and emotionally challenging time in a woman's life. Our well-being must be a top priority; otherwise we and our children will suffer.

A Mother of
Your Own Design

- Let this week be a call to action. Over the last few months, you've given birth, lost sleep, and rearranged your life to become a parent. It was difficult to catch your breath, let alone consider your own needs. Revisit the motherhood journal that you've been keeping. Are there some recurring themes? Are you in need of exercise? Friendship? Romance? Intellectual stimulation? A day alone? List the top three themes from your journal and three ways that you can remedy them. Take action.

- Most women feel "baby blues" or sadness in letting go of their old life in the first few weeks after birth. If you are depressed, or have visions of neglecting or harming your baby in any way, seek professional counseling immediately. Postpartum depression affects many women. If you're unable to get out of bed in the morning or carry on with daily routines, you need help. Ask a friend or family member to assist you in getting it.

Week 17

FRAGILE CREATIVITY

Listening and Responding to the Call

YOU DON'T HAVE TO be a writer or artist to understand the need for creativity. Some of us create in the kitchen, in the garden, or in a class. Many of us dabbled in creative pastimes before we had children, but integrating those activities with motherhood often feels difficult. We can list a barrage of reasons to let our creativity languish. My gifted painter friend can't imagine pulling out all of her supplies for only an hour of work at a time. "It seems worthless," she says, remembering lengthy afternoons at the canvas. She has never painted by the clock before. But then again, she has never stopped painting altogether either. She misses it terribly.

The creative spark is a mysterious calling, unsatisfied by anything other than listening and responding. It can come in the middle of the night, awakening us within the context of a dream. Sometimes it tiptoes into our thoughts as we're driving on the freeway or making the bed. Invariably it comes during the course of something else that we're doing, making it nearly impossible to stop, turn around, and run after it at that moment. No matter, just take note and make a promise to yourself to respond to this urge. Soon.

We all need time to listen, reflect, and act on our inner voice. Julia Cameron, author of *The Artist's Way,* puts it like this: "As an artist, I can literally die from boredom. I kill myself when I fail to nurture my artist child because I am acting like somebody else's idea of an adult.... Ignoring my artist means a grinding depression."

Nurturing your artist child when you're a mother is twice as difficult because you're tasked with nurturing another child, one who needs you sometimes more than you need yourself. Or so it seems. Family life is never finished. A baby requires attention and love around the clock. It is okay to step away sometimes, to surf to the promise of a creative wave. I glide back into motherhood after I've had a couple hours to chase words across the page, wondering where inspiration will finally take me. We're more than caregivers; we're full of ideas and dreams. I hope that you'll read these words and seek out the next creative urge that lands on your doorstep.

It's okay to hand off your baby to a caring "parent's day out" program for a morning of creativity. If you work full-time, dedicate a couple of lunch hours per week to your creative interests. Begin a ballet class, or pick up the pottery class that you took before the baby arrived. Look into the French lessons that you've always wanted to take. Listen to the inner artist whom you've ignored for too long. Our creativity is fragile, a flash of inspiration that we either record or watch fade away. These words, on the page before you, exist because I listened.

A Mother of
Your Own Design

- What are the ways in which you're creative? If you're unsure, think about the creative people whom you admire—famous or otherwise. Are you interested in similar pursuits?

- Keep your motherhood journal with you throughout the day for one week. When creative ideas present themselves, record them. At the end of the week, make a concise list of your ideas, and pursue the one that interests you most.

DEVOTION

Forging a Solitary Path

THE WORD *WORK* TAKES on another meaning when infused with the essence of devotion. Devotion compels us to act rather than nag. It's the smoothing of my daughter's curls when she's fighting a cold. Instinctively I comfort her, patting her back and easing her tears. I don't wager in my mind when it will end, or even if it will end. I do it because it is required. She has become one of the reasons that I walk this Earth. I am devoted to her, to nursing her back to health and watching her giggle at her brother.

Devotion temporarily disregards hunger and fatigue. Devotion's desire to console and soothe reaches beyond the constraints of our own needs. It is the strength that appears in the nick of time, the courage to trust our instincts, the love that summons us to stand guard watching. In the shadow of a career-oriented world, the act of calming a sick baby at three in the morning might seem small. It isn't.

There's little room to understand unless you've been there. We can try to explain it to coworkers who wonder why we've given up our twelve-hour days at the office, offering up as validation our heartfelt stories and revelations. But in the end we'll find that our devotion is a solitary journey. We need not justify it, nor defend it.

Eventually my daughter overcomes her bout with a virus. Like the first days of spring, when the snow begins to melt and the ground reappears, a smile returns to her face. Life bounds from her eyes as she reaches out to catch my hair in her fingers. I am at once grateful and ready to return to my routine again, to sleep more and eat whole meals sitting down.

Becoming a mother teaches us to choose consciously, perhaps for the first time. Our actions are governed less by the outside world and more by the soft whisper of love. Becoming a mother requires us to turn down the volume of the outside in order to hear the direction of our hearts. The ways that we walk through the day, consider our friends and family, and love our children are entirely up to us. Looking outside of ourselves doesn't bring us closer to the truth. Like an artist, we might model motherhood after our own upbringing, or perhaps after a trusted friend. But our interpretation will be different, new, and unique. Our devotion illumines the way.

A Mother of
Your Own Design

- List the ways you show devotion to your child. Read back over your list slowly, and post it on your bathroom mirror.

- Compliment a friend or family member for her work as a mother. Point out the ways in which she is devoted to her children.

Empty Mind

Claiming a Few Moments of Peace

THE PHONE RINGS, the infant video plays, the toys talk and sing songs. The baby cries, the dog barks, and someone knocks at the door to deliver a package. The newspaper lays lifelessly across the counter, unread. A new book sparkles beside the phone, its binding untouched. The day turns and weaves in and out of activity, until finally there's silence. Perhaps the baby is asleep, or on a walk with your partner. Only then a mother's thoughts return, as loud as the toys and television before them. They dart wildly from one subject to the next, pestering like bill collectors on overdue accounts. "Is there enough milk in the refrigerator for tomorrow? What time was that doctor's appointment on Friday? I'd like to play tennis."

Where do you go mentally and physically when suddenly you find yourself alone? A friend and I have discussed this many times, and neither one of us really knows what to do when silence enters the room. It's a jolt to stop running and responding to a baby's needs. For a few moments I walk around in a daze, trying to remember that I don't have to rinse out the bottles or stock diapers in the nursery. I'm free!

Yet my mind doesn't let me rest. It's begging for my attention as I shut the door to my study, the one place in our home that does not house toys, dolls, pacifiers, or blankies. As I begin to listen to my thoughts, time becomes my own again. In the quiet I can think like I used to, uninterrupted. Sometimes I write in my journal; other times I schedule plans on my calendar. As I listen, my thoughts relax. Thankfully, so do I. Writing things down allows me to become empty. My mental "To do" lists are like wallpaper that I strip nightly from the perimeter of my mind. I crave a blank slate, mental space to read a book, write a letter, or enjoy music. Sometimes I crave just the emptiness itself, to just be.

This process, of listening and emptying, is essential to our mental health. Caring for a baby requires every shred of consciousness. There is little room to coast, to breathe, to ruminate. Just when we've learned how to survive the first few weeks, our children require more of us. The baby's awake longer during the day and is determined to roll off the changing table. Our thoughts become preoccupied with meeting the next developmental milestone. We're easing transitions into child care, becoming vigilant about safety, and reading bedtime stories for better brain development. The stakes are so high!

This is precisely why we need silence every day, time to be available only to ourselves. We cannot walk around thinking about what we haven't done all of the time. Sometimes we need to slow the rumble of our thinking for a while, determine what's important and what we should let go. And then in the quiet that follows, we really are free. In my study at night, a candle burns steady and warm. The wind blows the trees beyond my window. I sink deeper into my chair and welcome myself like a long lost friend.

A Mother of
Your Own Design

* Is there a space in your home that is yours alone? Is it comforting? Finding a place of one's own does not require a separate room. It can be a nook, cordoned by a screen or a large piece of furniture. It can be a chair, a patch of earth, or a windowsill. Find a place that you can visit at the edges of your day. Give yourself time to retire there often.

- Endeavor to slow the chatter of your mind. Turn to your motherhood journal when your thoughts need to be heard. When you name your thoughts, it's easier to release them. Don't aim for eloquence. Just let the words leap onto the page freely. The purpose of keeping this journal is to listen and free ourselves from the meaningless, inviting our true selves back in the process.

MUSIC

Calling Upon a Muse

HIDDEN BENEATH THE notes of Beethoven's Piano Concerto No. 5 whispers a muse. Her words dangle in melody, a mélange of notes interpreted through the hands of a master composer. I borrow her inspiring verse from Beethoven himself, whenever I feel out of touch or control. The notes of a better world tumble upon me like raindrops in a forest—fully and softly falling from laden leaves. Music is a cachepot of grace, ebbing the flow of a bad day in an instant. I remember again who I am, who I really am. The convenient title of "mother" that I embrace so easily falls away. I am just trying to find my way like everyone else.

Music makes me feel less alone in my job of mothering. Through melody, the universe conspires to pull me to higher ground, letting me reflect upon where I've been. When you listen to music that tempers the soul, you'll notice a kinder day emerge between the notes. Music is a companion to guide you home, to the place where you're no longer caught in the drama of a fussy or sleepless afternoon. Music can lift you out of a fog to remember what's important, and then give you the will to respond. I often turn to Beethoven whenever a dose of higher wisdom is required.

If you'll think back over your life, you'll probably find that music has always played in the background. Beginning in your childhood, what songs played in your heart as you skipped with friends at recess? Do you remember the music that was played in your home as a child, and the instrument that you carried each morning to school? What singer's voices blared from your speakers while you were learning to drive? Remember the love songs that played on the radio in the weeks following your first kiss and heartbreak. A path of music winds around our years, weaving lyrics and notes into the texture of our most poignant memories. Despite the busyness of motherhood, don't neglect music.

Beethoven can turn on a dime to Raffi in my living room. "I've Been Working on the Railroad" has been known to follow a violin sonata, but that's motherhood— mixing a breath of inspiration with the commonplace. Raffi is anything but commonplace to my children, however. They sleep, eat, and drive happily to the sound of his voice singing childhood standards. Their lives are already intertwined with his musical refrains.

Are you feeling bored, tired, or frustrated? A good song will usually do the trick. Perhaps you'll dance around the house or lie down in the middle of a room. Music will transform your mood, make your soul sing. I wouldn't be the same mother without it, and neither will you.

A Mother of
Your Own Design

- Gather music from your past. As you listen to old songs, jot down memories in your motherhood journal. Remember who you were. Think of who you've become.

- Browse in an online music store. Listen to music samples and buy a new album that inspires you.

Literary Escape
Traveling the World in an Afternoon

Do you ever feel housebound? The weather might be whipping outside, or your baby might be sick with a cold. Whatever the condition, the walls of one's home can become confining at times. Rather than slink through the day, engage your fingertips and mind by opening a book. There must be at least one book on your shelf that has not yet been read. Perhaps there is even an old favorite that begs to be reread.

I escape often to Italy, France, and Spain, walking the landscapes of each and taking mental notes along the way. I must remember to return to Tuscany when the olives are harvested for oil. I love Provence when the lavender is lush upon the hills. I'd like to drive winding roads again in Andalucía, amidst lemon trees bending ripe with fruit.

Mental travelers need not pack diapers, snacks, or car seats. You're free to travel alone, which is even lighter.

, Frances Mayes, author of *Under the Tuscan Sun,* convinced me that I had not lived until I'd tried hazelnut gelato. She may have been right. I used her recipe one summer evening and passed it out to a bevy of grateful children and neighbors. On her many musings and expeditions into the Tuscan countryside, I tag along with her. I am her invisible companion while she peruses town markets looking for fresh vegetables and fruit. "Two weeks ago," she says, "small purple artichokes with long stems were in. We love those, quickly steamed, stuffed with tomatoes, garlic, yesterday's bread, and parsley, then doused with olive oil and vinegar."

In *Driving Over Lemons,* author Chris Stewart lures me to climb mountains with him on his sheep herding travails. "I took them up the hill to graze on the damp rosemary and thyme while I stood watching them through the wet mist, leaning on a crook. Below me wisps of cloud ebbed and flowed around the valley." I may be sitting in my kitchen, but my mind follows him through his Spanish countryside and a meadow of wild herbs.

When Peter Mayle describes the experience of French cafés in *Encore Provence,* I am sitting at a small table on the edge of a cobblestone street. "You are expected to linger," he says. "You can read a newspaper, write a love letter, daydream, plan a coup d'état or use the café as an office." All I can think about is the luxury of an empty afternoon to sit at my café, eavesdropping on the banter of patrons and writing in my journal.

It's refreshing to roam the world—plunging into different countries, meeting new people and tasting their cuisine. If walking another step in your home leaves you less than inspired, sashay into a well-told story. The charms of being at home return after sampling new horizons. Books are an open invitation to another place and time. A baby will usually allow you to sneak a few pages throughout the day. Good books lead us to discover that it is not our house that binds us, but rather the dullness of our thoughts. Reading refreshes the mind and the imagination.

A Mother of
Your Own Design

- Put all of your parenting books aside for a week; yes, even this one. You've culled enough information about parenting to write a doctoral dissertation. Select a book to read for pleasure. Place it on your nightstand, in the kitchen, or in the nursery. Keep it on hand for empty moments.

- In your motherhood journal, start a running list of books that you'd like to read. Visit the library, go to the bookstore, or swap favorites with a friend. If you're inclined, start or join a book club.

Mother's Day

Celebrating It for the First Time

IT'S THE STUFF OF POETRY—good and, well, store-
bought. Honor your mother, all of her hard work and
dedication. Honor the way she cares for you when you're
sick and well. Honor the way she has dedicated her life to
you. Mother's Day is probably a holiday perpetuated more
by the greeting card industry than by children, yet we
wouldn't miss it. Mom deserves a bouquet of daisies, or
at least a handful of purple clover plucked from a nearby
field. She'll place them in a canning jar on the windowsill,
admiring them as long as they last. It's a rare day, being
celebrated as a mother.

For my first Mother's Day, my husband crafted a card
for me in childlike handwriting, a surrogate love letter

from my three-month-old son. We dined out and brought home a video for dessert. We started our movie and placed our son in his swing, bathed and dressed for bed. Five minutes into the movie, I noticed two eyes staring at me. My son's favorite toy sat on the tray in front of him, but he wasn't interested. Television images and the window next to him didn't hold his attention either. He had turned his head to watch me.

The movie's dialogue grew faint as I scooped him out of his swing and pulled him to me. His feathery blond hair brushed my chin and he nestled into the arc of my neck. The movie, the living room, and the night fell away. My love for him is as involuntary as his attachment to me. For me, Mother's Day is a celebration of the sublime bond that exists between a mother and her child.

Mother's Day began in the United States as a day dedicated to peace. In 1872, Julia Ward Howe penned a "Mother's Day Proclamation" that called for disarmament and an end to war. Her stirring words, surely inspired by her love for her children, moved many women to convene in Boston annually to promote peace.

We credit our current Mother's Day to Anna Jarvis of Philadelphia, who led a massive campaign to adopt a formal holiday to honor all mothers, living and departed. Her campaign began as a memorial to her own mother, who in the late nineteenth century had established "Mother's

Friendship Days" to encourage healing from the loss of life incurred during the Civil War. In 1914, President Woodrow Wilson officially proclaimed Mother's Day as a national holiday to be held on the second Sunday of May. Less than ten years later, Jarvis watched sadly as a wave of commercialization swept over the holiday. Mother's Day no longer held the meaning that she wished for it. "This is not what I intended," she said. "I wanted it to be a day of sentiment, not profit!"

In honor of Anna Jarvis, may your first Mother's Day be rich in sentiment. Cards, chocolates, and flowers are lovely, but a mother's real treasure is found in the loving gaze of her baby's eyes.

A Mother of *Your Own Design*

- Begin a family tradition for Mother's Day. Find a way to celebrate simply, reflecting on the wonder of maternal love and devotion. Schedule a day trip to a botanical garden, or tell the story of the day your child was born. You might feel inclined to take up the banner of peace, like Julia Ward Howe, marching in a parade or writing to Congress.

- Honor your own mother in a meaningful way, whether she is living or dead. You might write a note of appreciation, plant a rose bush, or say a prayer for her. We learn to appreciate our mothers more after having our own children. Even if your relationship with your mother is not what you'd like it to be, find a way to honor her for the gift of your life.

WORK IS NO LUXURY
You Don't Need a Job to Take a Break

S O LIFE HAS BECOME a bit more normal. Perhaps your life is even predictable at times, a blessing considering how many months you struggled with sleep and not knowing when your next break during the day would come. We cling to these schedules, eking out a few more chores before the baby wakes. We busy ourselves during naptimes, knowing it's our only hope of balancing the checkbook or cleaning the bathroom. We might even begin to believe working is a luxury, a way to take a break from parenting while still contributing to the family. It's easier to break from parenting when we can hang our hat on another "productive" activity.

A friend expressed mixed emotions to me about returning to her job while her baby was still young. "I feel so guilty. I wanted to stay home with him but now I want to work to get away from him. It sounds so terrible," she says.

We don't need an excuse to get away from parenting for a while, even a well-meaning one like work. Certainly some of us will need or want to work. There are others of us who go back to the office simply to get away. When we don't value the nature of our work as mothers, we have trouble admitting that as with any profession, we too need vacation, sick days, and holidays. We would never accept employment with the conditions that we willingly accept as mothers—working 24 hours a day without pay. Under these working conditions, why wouldn't we need to get away sometimes?

"They're only children. We should be better than that. We're their mothers," you might interject. We are their mothers, but when did we cross over the mortal threshold and become perfect? Was it when we walked out of the hospital with the baby in our arms or at the moment of conception? Let's demystify the word *mother*, and perhaps we'll become more comfortable with just taking a break every once in a while. It's okay to seek out solace in conversation with a friend over lunch weekly. It's even okay to go away for a night by yourself to enjoy a good novel and a full night's sleep. Let go of your dutiful ways; let down your guard and just live a little!

A Mother of
Your Own Design

- How do you define your work in the world? Does it include the work of mothering? Don't discount the life energy and time you give to your child.

- Think about the ways you can build regular breaks into your mothering schedule. This will probably require some assistance from others. Ask for it. Trade for it or pay for it. Require it of yourself, as you would any responsibility. You deserve it.

Who Are You?

Letting Go of the Need to Compare

With a new baby, developmental milestones are big news. Sometime during those early weeks, you notice that small face unexpectedly smiling up at you. Despite the hour or task at hand, the first grin can send you reeling like your first kiss in the eighth grade. Perhaps the earliest landmark in a baby's growth, a first smile hints at delights to follow. We get a glimpse of a burgeoning personality, a small person with preferences and aptitude. It doesn't take long before that personality emerges, nor long before we respond to it. She's a talker. He's a flirt. She loves the outdoors. He's such a boy!

We wait and watch, recording their development along the way. Sometimes we compare notes with other mothers. "Has he rolled over yet? Mine rolled onto her stomach last night." We sometimes prod and analyze our baby's development, hurrying and worrying. "Surely, she will crawl by seven months. How will she learn to walk by ten months if she's not crawling soon?" All of this analysis has one effect, and that is to feel as though your baby is not living up to someone else's expectations. And let's extend that further—to your own.

You may read libraries of books on development in the first year, and believe me, I did. But in the end, your baby is unique. She will walk when she's ready, and she might not even crawl beforehand. My daughter dragged herself around the house like a seal for months before she realized her legs could help her to crawl. I tried to focus on her upper-body strength instead of bemoaning her "delayed" development. Since she was my second child, it was easier. When she did walk, she rarely fell. She grew according to her own needs, not mine, and not those listed in the charts of my books.

Letting our babies develop in their own time might be easier written than done. Certainly there are times to be worried, to consult with the pediatrician. Mostly though, this is an elemental exercise in trust. When a six-month-old turns his nose up at all food other than breast milk, trust that he will get over it. Don't worry too much. He'll be just fine. Of course the same goes for those little personalities, the likes and dislikes that seem to emerge from nowhere. Our children come into this world with their own inclinations. Let's trust them to show us who they are, and perhaps most important, let's trust ourselves to embrace them when they do.

A Mother of
Your Own Design

- Spend some time this week noticing the ways in which your baby expresses herself. She might push applesauce away, for example, but does she love peaches? Is there a way that you can honor her likes while still giving her the nutrition that she needs? Motherhood is easier when we work with rather than against our children.

- Whenever you feel drawn into a conversation that gauges or evaluates a baby's development, stop yourself. Offer words of support and trust. Our babies are going to grow according to their needs, not ours.

BREAKING DOWN

Reaching Out to a Mother in Need

I WITNESSED A MOTHER breaking down today. She lost it in front of eight children, three mothers, and a teacher. Frustration, anger, and tears burst from a veneer of composure. She was living beyond her limit, pushed to an edge that I recognized immediately. I was on the other side of the classroom when it happened, picking up my son. Tentatively I walked over to where she stood, listening to her as she talked and cried about her baby—how much she and her husband had wanted him, and what a challenge he had been since he was born. Now he was a busy eight-month-old, full of opinions and energy. His fighting spirit often felt too much for her to handle. When he was an infant, his temperament was equally challenging. Perhaps he cried a lot and only slept a little. Perhaps he was a picky eater. Perhaps his perpetual fussiness made it difficult for her to feel as though she was doing a good job.

Guilt ridden, she needed us to listen. She needed to know that she was not alone with her fears and frustration. One mother looked shocked at first, unsure how to respond to her sudden emotion. We're not usually called to help one another in this sort of real way. We say our hellos and good-byes every morning, but rarely are we called on to lend a strong shoulder. There is a mythology about motherhood that is perpetuated when we pretend always to have it under control. We see other mothers whose clothes are ironed, whose kids are well behaved, whose cars are cleaner. Their countenance seems calmer than ours, and we secretly long for their skill. Today I realized that one of the mothers I've admired is just as human as I am. Maybe she believed that we had answers that she was lacking. The truth is we're all struggling, trying to do our best. None of us is that perfect mother in the sky.

So how do we know our efforts are not going to waste, especially when our child's behavior doesn't meet our expectations? The effects of our hard work might take years to realize, but there are flashes of breakthrough along the way. You've seen it when you expect it least. A strong-willed ten-month-old lovingly kisses her doll, patting it on the back and wrapping it in a blanket. A six-week-old infant with a penchant for screaming smiles at his parents for the first time. We need to remain aware and cherish these moments when they occur. They are signposts, encouraging us to persevere in spite of the difficulties.

Of course, a mother needs more than mere moments. She needs a friend to lean on in the trying times. We all know those times; they occur daily. What good does it do us to pretend that they don't? Opportunities to reach out to other mothers present themselves all of the time. On airplanes, tired mothers walk up and down aisles with crying babies. Could we offer our arms if they're free for a few minutes? In grocery stores, mothers push demanding children in carts packed with a week's worth of food. Could we pass along an encouraging comment, or at least a smile of sympathy? Although our lives might be just as busy, it takes very little to help, encourage, and support.

Motherhood is not a walk in the park, nor is it an eighteen-year sentence. It is a lot like running a marathon. You have to pace yourself, and you have to be in good condition to see the race through. You also need people handing you water along the way.

A Mother of
Your Own Design

- Pay attention to the mothers who frequent your circle of living. Say hello to them in passing. Offer them assistance when they need it.

- Pass along helpful articles, books, and contacts to other mothers. Share your experiences.

A SETTLING EXPERIENCE

Recognizing the Distance You've Traveled

SOONER OR LATER it happens. You'll see a mother carrying her brand-new baby and you'll realize how far you've come. She's walking from the car to the grocery store, carrying her infant in soft pink blankets that are still new and fluffy. She's visibly tired, uncombed and clumsy while placing her car seat in the grocery cart. The baby sleeps or cries, and either way, she hurries down the aisles to dash back home. If the baby sleeps, I always want to say, "Enjoy it; relax." But I know my words would fall to the floor, only to be swept up by the boys who stock the shelves later in the afternoon.

The voyage into motherhood is solitary, and usually our learning is not hastened by the good intentions of family, friends, in-laws, or complete strangers in Safeway.

It's best to let a new mother cut her own trail, allowing her the hands-on experience she needs before plying her with helpful hints. There's nothing like a few busy months of caring for an infant to knock you closer to proficiency. And that's where we find ourselves now, suddenly more adept in the day-to-day care of our children.

I remember a time when I couldn't fathom taking care of my infant and cooking dinner in a ten-hour day. How would I nurse, soothe, and boil pasta? Impossible!

Take some time to retrace your steps, to appreciate the progress you've made as a mother. You've accomplished it; you're already halfway through the first year, and your baby is growing, learning, and thriving. The physical stamina and emotional endurance you've developed—through childbirth, on-demand breastfeeding, and sleep deprivation—have redefined you. You're stronger now, perhaps more confident in handling the unexpected fever that registers in the middle of the night. You may no longer need your hand held during your baby's vaccinations. A friend just told me that she has mastered nursing inconspicuously while standing in line to renew her driver's license. Forget about boiling pasta! We have reinvented ourselves in the last six months, looping our children into the nap of daily living.

Lest you gloss over the magnitude of this accomplishment, take an afternoon to honor your maternal self. Celebrate this six-month milestone. You deserve it.

A Mother of
Your Own Design

- Read back over the first few weeks of your motherhood journal. Remember how difficult those early weeks were, and recognize how far you've come as a mother.

- Make a list of your maternal qualities of which you're most proud.

It's the Small Things

Packing More Than Just Formula

CONVENIENCE COULD not be more important than when you're juggling a baby and all of his gear. Life away from home—whether you're traveling long distances or just running errands—requires the diaper bag, a soft portable container that despite its size barely carries everything required for a day away. We pack the diapers, wipes, changing pad, diaper cream or powder, bags for disposal, formula, bottles, burp cloths, cold packs, nutritious snacks, baby food, little spoons, bibs, blankets, change of clothes, and toys to occupy. There might be a small corner in the side pocket for your wallet and keys, but that's it. "I'll catch lunch on the road," you might say, which might mean fast food and a soda.

Does any of this seem unbalanced? We have enough time to ensure mobile refrigeration, but how often do we pack ourselves a nutritious lunch? How can we be more responsive to ourselves and to the ingredients that we require during the day?

I have a theory about this inequity. We don't think about packing anything for ourselves because there's no more room left in the diaper bag. Obviously then, to grant ourselves parity, we need another bag. Another bag? It's difficult enough to haul around this small kitchen pantry, you might say. We could get a larger diaper bag, but would it still fit under the seat in front of us or in an overhead bin? Don't worry; ours will be much smaller and lighter. It might be a purse, only more utilitarian.

We pack our children diced fruit. We could do the same for ourselves. We pack diaper cream for their comfort. We could pack hand cream for ourselves. We could bring a bottle of water, another shirt for ourselves (for the same accident that requires our baby's change of clothes), and a book to read during unexpected naps.

Keeping a bag stocked just for us is an inexpensive, easy way to care for ourselves. We might dream about regular massage appointments and facials, but it's the small things that cushion us throughout the day—warm gloves for nippy evenings, and sunglasses for bright mornings. Extend your maternal self by allowing her to consider your every need. She'll pack you a lunch, slip a few bills into your wallet, and surprise you with a couple of chocolate kisses for dessert. Let her pack your bag with as much foresight and love as she does your child's diaper bag. Your days away from home will be much sweeter.

A Mother of
Your Own Design

- In your motherhood journal, make a list of the items that would make your days away from home easier. Don't worry about weight or quantity. You can edit it down later. Your list might include lip balm, perfumed hand lotion, bottled water, a brush and hair clip, quarters, an apple, protein bars, mints, a cellular phone, stamps, emergency phone numbers, a small calendar, and so on.

- Find a compact bag in your closet, or buy one, to load with your necessities. Keep it in the car so that you'll always have it on hand.

Vacation

Swimming into Summer

Have you taken a vacation lately? It's time to put up your feet and relax. Take a good book, the one that has been sitting on your nightstand untouched. Invite good friends or family members to join you, if you choose. Where should you go? Select someplace close if you can; don't be burdened by extensive travel. Babies and parents are happier on short trips. Take the necessities. Leave the rest behind.

When summer comes, I look forward to the roll of water on a wide beach. Sea breezes curl my hair and waves bubble at my toes. I walk at sunrise, leaving a trail of tiny puddles glistening behind me. Late in the afternoon, I run my fingers through warm shallow pools left by the tide. My daughter sits in my lap watching her brother run through a fleeting lagoon. He and a new playmate are trudging happily, knee-deep in water and bliss. My husband has drifted off, dreaming in the shadow of an umbrella. Our summer vacation has begun.

We return to the ocean each year, without the weight of schedules and work. The phone never rings, and clocks go unnoticed. We fall asleep when we're tired and eat when we're hungry. We ride bikes in the evenings after dinner. The days drift simply, marvelously empty and full.

I often wonder how I might cultivate this kind of leisure at home. Our days seem too invested in speed and activity. We live by a calendar, our freedom found between the scribbles of appointments and plans. We drive, work, volunteer, cook, and console—and in between we change diapers and stock the refrigerator. At the end of the day, we shuffle through the mail, pay bills, and add another newspaper to the recycling basket. When we wake up, we'll do it again and again and again.

But not today. Let the days of summer cool your heels, in spite of July heat. Respite might be found in a stretch of beach, a mountain lake, or a campsite in the woods. Wherever your soul beckons, follow. Readjust to a leisurely pace. Slow your thoughts to the rhythm of nature. Summer vacations mark our lives like the passing of time, striking another memory in our little history, adding a couple pages to the family album. Planning it and anticipating it are half the fun. When winter temperatures cool the windowpanes, and landscapes turn bleak, plan a vacation. When sunshine and warmth flood through the house months later, pack your bags and load up the car. Swim in the idea of summer.

A Mother of
Your Own Design

* When was the last time that your family took a vacation? After a baby enters the home, the thought of vacationing is never as spontaneous as it once was. There is the high chair, the portable bassinet, the car seat, the stroller, and that's not even counting the toys that entertain and occupy. No matter. Pare it down where you can and find a way to bring what you think you'll need. Then, let your mind think of more interesting pursuits, like the strolls you'll take on the beach with your family.

* Include grandparents on summer vacations. They'll love spending time with their grandchild, and you might be able to negotiate a little time with your husband to dine out or sleep in together.

WHAT ABOUT ME?

Widening Our Focus

THERE COMES A TIME during the first year when one's ambitions return—activities, hopes, and dreams that predated the birth of our babies. They might be professional, athletic, creative, or social pursuits—getting a promotion, running a 5K, writing a book, or spending more time with old friends. When our aspirations return, we've usually mastered the fundamentals of babyhood. We're more competent at juggling, feeding, and nurturing. But how well are we nurturing ourselves?

Many women give up on themselves in the first year, perhaps not realizing it as it happens. It can be compelling to be needed so completely. Our days are full, and it's so easy to let our interests wane. An athletic friend of mine ran miles each morning before her baby was born. She and her husband took bicycle trips that lasted three days, savoring the countryside from a slower pace. She competed in triathlons and lived an active, adventurous life before she had children. It has been five years since her daughter was born, but she rarely runs or bikes anymore. Motherhood fills up her days, takes all of her energy, and competes for her attention even when she's away. Lately she has begun to remember who she was before her child was born. In the moments between dreams and consciousness, she longs to feel her feet on the road—carrying her through the early mist of morning.

Resuming the exact life we lived before children is impossible. Motherhood changes us. We have to be present for our children, but let's not forget ourselves along the way. Let's pay attention to the Self that calls to us from dreams. If we don't listen to the urging of our soul, how will we teach our children to recognize the longing of theirs? Caring for another is not always an act of subjugating the self. We can't give up exploring and uncovering what's authentic for us. Obligation can lead to martyrdom, and a life of "have to" leaves us numb. We must not fall off the Earth just because we're mothers. We'll give more purposefully when we remain available to ourselves—staying open to the questions, mysteries, and insights revealed in pre-dawn sleep. Our lives are big enough to absorb the curiosity of our wonderings, and the wonderings of our children.

I think about my friend in the early morning, imagine her skimming over green hills by foot. Her breath hangs on the air as her legs carve through a fog that rises from a nearby lake. She's smiling, peaceful, and ready for a new day.

A Mother of
Your Own Design

- Catch your dreams quickly in the mornings. Write them down before they become fuzzy in the light of dawn. Do you notice any themes? What are they asking of you?

- Only you know the ways that you neglect the call of your Self. What have you been longing to do lately? Do it, or some part of it, this week. Try not to judge yourself. Just enjoy.

INNOCENCE

Living Our First Life

HAVE YOU EVER noticed that a baby rarely hesitates? Caution lives in a different universe. A baby will accept the world as it comes to him, because he has no experiences that tint or translate the moment he occupies. Life flows freely over him, waves of events untouched by expectation. When does the tendency to interpret and evaluate life happen? Is it with language, or perhaps with memory?

Somewhere along the line, we develop a second life, one that lives in tandem to the first. It shadows us through inner dialogue, a streaming conversation that stirs and dilutes our experiences, changing them into something we understand or assume. The second self lives quietly, almost invisibly, behind the scenes.

Imagine an early summer morning, sitting in a green field. Have you watched a baby touching grass, or observing sunlight bounce through trees? His world is present, tactile, and fascinating. He's captivated, filled with the activity around him. He turns to the sound of birds chirping in a bush behind him, and looks up to observe an airplane in the sky. A mother sitting next to him might also hear the birds and see the plane, but their presence is secondary in her consciousness.

I should have put sunscreen on him before we came outside. I always forget his sunscreen and hat. There's a plane. He likes planes. Maybe I should buy him a book on airplanes.

Her random run-on thinking pollutes the present. She can't see the plane because she is not really looking at it. It is like a word in a book memorized by sight; reading it feels unnecessary. She moves on. The baby stops, looks, and sees. She moves through an internal landscape instead of enjoying the one before her. Her eyes are open, but she sees very little.

Too often, we miss the sanctity of the present. The present usually arrives peacefully, offering itself as a refuge over and over again while we sit muddled in our minds. We might believe that our thoughts are productive or even interesting, but we're really ignoring the gift of the day before us.

This is where our children can teach us. Babies absorb the world around them, touching, tasting, and seeing.

They delight in their senses, enjoying the unexpected swoop of a robin or the warmth of the sun emerging from a cloud. Let's suspend our thinking for a change, return to the simple and original mind with which we were born. Let's immerse ourselves in the river of the senses—to drift, swim, and float in the day.

A Mother of *Your Own Design*

- Practice present moment awareness. Take five minutes and observe your life. You might be juggling activities in the middle of an afternoon, or watching the moon ascend from a bedroom window. Wherever you are, bring your awareness to the moment at hand and take it all in. When competing thoughts enter your mind, acknowledge them without engaging in them. Bring yourself gently back to the present.

- When you feel worried about the future, or mired in some aspect of the past, practice present-moment awareness to regain a sense of balance and peace.

Week 31

BECOMING FREE

Surrendering the Ego

I'VE BECOME FREER since having a baby. I may not get to the movies or linger in conversation with girl-friends as much, but I have tasted a freedom that was foreign to me before having children. It didn't come without a price, mind you, but freedom rarely does. I've learned to abandon my ego, surrender it to two little people who need me more. I wish I could say that I had a hand in this accomplishment, but in fact, it's impossible not to surrender that part of us when caring for a baby. Who can be self-absorbed with a baby in their care? The responsibility always takes you away from yourself, gets you out of your skin. The physical demands preclude our egocentric predilections during the day. There's little time to be preoccupied with oneself when a baby's life requires so much attention and maintenance. Personally, I have very little time to obsess over my relationships, career, or appearance. Having a baby streamlines old anxieties, simplifies what's important, and discards the rest.

What a relief! Does anyone else feel this way? Perhaps it's a secret benefit to motherhood, silently celebrated in the cloistered emotional lives of mothers. I don't have to be eternally eighteen, wear a size 2, make a million dollars, or solve the world's most pressing problems. I still find these things appealing, but really, life is easier when you just live it instead of wishing it were different.

I am content gazing into the eyes of my children. I love them unconditionally, a quality of acceptance I've seldom granted myself. The idea that they might be better in the future or more acceptable when they achieve something is absurd to me. I love them wholeheartedly as they are now, as they'll be next week and next year. Oh sure, I'd like my son to eat at least one vegetable on the planet, and I'd like my daughter to stop standing in grocery carts. But these are the details that curve and twist the branches of our family tree. After all, we are simply who we are.

The ego tells us who we "should" be. It's the voice that asks us to betray our real self, to defy what's authentic for us. It's the antithesis of reason, the worry that keeps us up at night. The ego teases with promises of happiness if we could only be something different from what we are.

My children have shown me that the more engaged in

life I am—body, mind, and soul—the happier I am. I have less time to listen to that voice of unreason, its judgmental whisperings. We love our children easily for who they are, and maybe along this road we will find that same comforting affection for ourselves.

A Mother of
Your Own Design

- Notice the ways you love your child and the ways you love yourself. How are they similar? Different?

- What standards of the ego are you holding onto? Are you withholding any acceptance from yourself for not being the person you think you "should" be?

PROGRESS

Longing for the Kitchen

OUR PROGRESS AS women, noticeable in our paychecks and careers, wavers after having children. I'm not referring to inadequate maternity or paternity leave, expensive or substandard child care, or even the fact that "working" mothers statistically continue to do the majority of housework. I'm talking about something simpler, a need that most of us feel whether we're home with our children or working away from them. That is the need for a community—for a circle of mothers whom we might rely upon, learn from, and turn to.

I often crave mornings spent in someone else's kitchen, sharing a cup of coffee and conversation. I long for a next-door companion to ease the day, whose children might play with my own. Perhaps what I crave is another time, my mother's time. She sat in our kitchen with a good friend who lived nearby, sharing soda on hot Virginia afternoons and shooing kids into the backyard. She, like most of our neighbors who were mothers, did not work outside the home. She took ballet classes a couple nights a week and read books during the day. I know that she did not have enough time to herself and probably didn't feel justified in asking for it. She lived as most of the women in her generation lived around her.

When we think about progress for women, we usually recognize the opportunities that we have professionally. When we think about progress for mothers, we typically recognize our fortune in choosing a career, motherhood, or both. Rarely do we consider the quality of our lives in making those choices. Although we've gained opportunities that contribute to our own growth, we've given up something else too dear, something that nourished generations of mothers before us. Where are our maternal communities?

Yes, there are "playgroups" organized for new mothers, weekly gatherings that allow new babies and mothers a chance to convene. There are music and movement classes. Public libraries offer weekly story time, half-hour sessions where mothers and babies befriend other mothers and babies. But for the most part, maternal communities rely more upon self-initiative and less upon geography.

I am not lacking in self-initiative, but this mother mourns old neighborhoods brimming with kids, mothers, and unlocked front doors. It seems extreme to suggest, as many do, that women must give up their professional pursuits in order to enjoy a more cohesive maternal community.

Perhaps we are required to leave a little time in our days to reach out to the mother who lives next to us. Maybe she is just as lonely and overscheduled as we are. After a long day at the office, she might jump at the chance to feed her family alongside ours, a lasagna dinner in the backyard. Perhaps we could share a cup of herbal tea in her kitchen after the babies are asleep. I might bring the tea bags and she might supply the cups. It only takes a moment to ask, and a few minutes to boil the water.

A Mother of *Your Own Design*

- Whether you stay at home or work outside the house, consider the ways that you can connect with mothers who live near you. Invite a neighbor to go on a twenty-minute morning walk, or form a dinner co-op with a few mothers in the neighborhood.

- Trade babysitting with mothers in your neighborhood. You'll get to know your neighbors quickly while caring for each other's children.

BEDTIME

Turning In

THERE IS ONE CONSTANT in early motherhood that shades the course of our days. If we get enough of it, our days feel vibrant. If we don't, our days drag and pull us along. By now, I don't have to tell you that getting enough sleep at night during the first year of motherhood is a challenge akin to climbing Mt. Everest. Few souls manage it; most of us peter out at base camp.

According to the National Sleep Foundation, new mothers lose up to 700 hours of sleep in the first year—one month's worth of sleep. You know the effects of too little rest: dark circles under the eyes, shortened temper and attention span. Sleeplessness is epidemic in America, but women and especially mothers fare the worst.

I could take a nap right now. That is, if I didn't have to

work, take the cat to the vet, and pick up my children from a friend's house. And then I really would get to bed earlier, if my husband and I didn't have to clean up all of the toys strewn from our mailbox to the edge of our backyard. There are clean dishes to stack in cupboards and bottles to fill with milk. Junk mail clutters the countertops and crumbs lay underneath.

You know what I'm referring to—the endless array of tasks that would go unfinished if you took an afternoon nap or went to bed at a decent hour. Well, as it turns out, every time we choose the dishes over our beds, we're compromising our health. Scientists have discovered that sleep is as important to longevity as healthy eating and regular exercise. We age more quickly without sleep and are at greater risk for health problems, including heart attacks and breast cancer. There is even a study that suggests prolonged sleep deprivation can lead to thicker waistlines, due to a slowed production of hormones that regulate the craving for carbohydrates and the body's proportion of fat to muscle. As if we needed another card stacked against us in the uphill climb to reclaim our pre-pregnancy bodies!

The point is, our sleep is not optional. We're awakened enough as it is; let's not make the situation worse by cheating ourselves when we can get it. Restful nights are never guaranteed with a baby. We should chase sleep when we can. The unfinished projects piling up are tempting. So is slumber.

Clean sheets tumble warm in the dryer. What if my husband and I left this mess, climbed into bed, and buried ourselves in blankets? We'd have a mess to clean in the morning, but then we'd have a mess to clean in just a few hours anyway.

The moments before drifting off to sleep are some of the sweetest of the day. The day's difficulties soften and succumb to the call of something stronger and restorative. We might fight it initially, as children often do, but the urge to sleep cloaks us like a thick quilt. Its warmth lulls us deeper. Ask your body what it really wants, and I'd wager you'll be smoothing those sheets and pulling up the covers in no time.

A Mother of
Your Own Design

- Good sleep habits require discipline. Make your sleep a priority by going to bed at the same hour, even on the weekends. If you're a night owl but your children wake up at the crack of dawn, prepare for bed earlier in the night. Take a warm bath, practice breathing or relaxation exercises. Avoid caffeine, cigarettes, alcohol, and exercise before bedtime. If possible, take a nap when your baby sleeps during the day. According to sleep experts, 20 minutes will refresh you as much as an hour.

- If your baby is still not sleeping through the night at six months, find a book that will assist you in encouraging him to sleep. Babies need "sleep cues" to help them transition into sleep, just like adults do.

Fairy-Tale Families

Refining the Dream

Each of us carries around a fantasy when it comes to family life, an idealized version of our own childhood or sometimes its shining opposite. While we're pregnant, it grows with the baby; we imagine ways to emulate it and bring it into reality. We envision "happily ever after" days that we'll enjoy after becoming parents. In our minds, we're pushing a baby carriage and sauntering through images dressed in fine Irish linen. Only after having a baby do we realize how rumpled and wrinkled motherhood can be. If the first weeks of motherhood don't refine the fairy tale, the months that follow surely do.

Our earliest fantasies about motherhood house many expectations. It's up to us to question those images and designs that our psyches still demand of us. It's probably not reasonable to wish that our homes will always be spotless, or that our babies will always behave. What June Cleaver vacuuming-in-pearls image do you carry around in your mind?

Even with the dawn of feminism in the '60s and '70s, the 1950s model of motherhood still resonates with many of us. We know intellectually that it isn't authentic or equitable, so what do we possibly gain by holding onto that image? There is something noble about unwavering dedication and love. Could it be possible that we endeavor to become something we need ourselves—an unconditional loving presence that nurtures, protects, and supports us? Perhaps we long for someone who will wait at home for us, bake warm cookies for us, and shelter us from stormy weather.

William Makepeace Thackeray said, "Mother is the name of God in the lips and hearts of children." As adults, are we aligning motherhood with the work of God? Or perhaps, are we confusing ourselves with God? Our quest to become the ideal mother might really be a call for the Divine in our own lives. A higher wisdom often infuses our work as mothers, but we are not perfect. We need the same love and care that our children do.

Little else in our culture is as sacred as motherhood. We undervalue our teachers, look hard for esteemed leaders, and pick apart our heroes. Yet there is an aura that still follows mothers, an impenetrable light that we try hard to earn. But just as our heroes, leaders, and teachers are human beings, so are mothers. We have moments of inspiration, brushes with Wisdom, and we also have moments that are pretty mediocre. That's the catch, the paradoxical hue of motherhood. We're blessed with the work of heaven while we're living here, like everyone else, on Earth.

A Mother of *Your Own Design*

- What is your fantasy about motherhood? Take inventory of the ways you sabotage yourself with unrealistic expectations.

- Are you trying to give your baby something that you feel is lacking in your life? If so, how can you nurture those orphaned aspects of yourself? Through a chosen faith? Through relationships with friends, mentors, or family members? Through creative pursuits?

Week 35

Moments of Frustration

Cleaning Up and Moving On

WHOM DO YOU lean on in times of frustration or uncertainty? Is it your spouse or a best friend? It might be your mother or father. We all need support along this path—sage advice or simply a nod of understanding.

One of my biggest challenges during the first year was coping with a skill that my son developed to protest certain foods, naps, and even bedtime. To protest peas, for example, he would throw up on demand. It seems extreme, I know. He didn't seem to mind; in fact, he preferred throwing up to ingesting one small mashed pea. Not wanting him to repeat the behavior, I moved on to the next vegetable and the next, and eventually decided to give up altogether. At least he liked fruit. The first time it happened, I thought he had a stomach virus. As it turns out, he really didn't mind gagging to tell me that he didn't like something.

Soon, he was gagging at naptime and at bedtime. I have cleaned more crib rails, sheets, and carpets than I care to remember. I was desperate for him to stop; my books offered little advice and my days felt like drudgery. Even my mother was perplexed.

Perhaps all mothers have a time like this, when you stare at your baby and think to yourself, "What have I gotten myself into?" There are no guarantees that he'll behave the way we want him to.

I wish I could tell you that I found an answer to this problem. I could only change my response to him, since I couldn't change his behavior. Getting angry didn't work, and I obviously couldn't ignore his behavior. I just had to clean up and move on. The key for me was in the second part—moving on. I had no control over when my son would throw up, but I was going to be sure that it didn't ruin me for the rest of the day.

I also confessed to my best friend my shame in having a nine-month-old who knew how to push my buttons in the most frustrating way I could imagine. "Whose baby does this?" I asked. She listened and consoled me, understanding my disappointment without judging my son or me. The truth is that all children surprise, scare, and baffle their mothers eventually. I was fortunate to have someone who listened to my fears and loved me in spite of them.

I don't remember how long my son's defiance-by-vomit continued, but it wasn't short-lived. In a strange way, it prepared me as his mother more than the duller moments. He tested and strengthened my patience, and somehow I continue to love him fiercely.

A Mother of
Your Own Design

- Who listens to you, believes in you, and trusts you as a mother? It's important to have a confidant, someone who will hear your frustrations without judgment. Sometimes a family member might be too emotionally attached to you and your child to offer unconditional support.

- How does your child challenge you? How can you "clean up and move on"? Visualize a better way to handle a frustrating situation while preserving your peace of mind.

In Search of Rejuvenation

Taking the Day Off

How long has it been since you've taken the day off? I'm referring to the whole day, not two hours in a shopping mall. If your baby's eating solid foods and drinking from a cup or bottle, this is your chance. What would you do with yourself for a whole day alone? Take some time to think about it; the ideas will come to you quickly.

Hiking in a state park might fit the bill, staring up at the sky through limbs and leaves. Take plenty of water and a picnic lunch to enjoy along the way. If the weather won't permit, visit your favorite museum. Pay for a guided tour and learn something new. Have a long lunch at your favorite restaurant and bring a book if you're hesitant about dining alone. Drink a glass of your favorite wine, and enjoy being served. If you live near the beach, spend time by the shore. Collect shells, meditate to the rhythm of the waves, snorkel with the fish. Abandon motherhood for a day and engage yourself in something interesting.

You might be sailing with me on the idea of being free for a day, but a series of objections are forming on your lips as you traipse mentally down a mountain trail. Who will watch the baby? Will my child cry for me while I'm gone? Is it right to leave for a whole day when I'm not even going to work?

Trust me; you need this. You both need a break. By now you should know that we're better mothers when we've had some time to ruminate in our thoughts and revel in the outside world for a change.

For my first whole day away from motherhood, I drove to the city for a morning of art and an afternoon of "high tea." While browsing Picasso's lesser-known drawings, I listened to a string quartet that formed unexpectedly in the museum's lobby. At tea, I nibbled on cucumber sandwiches and miniature French pastries. I sipped English Breakfast tea from china and relaxed into an armchair covered in tapestry, accompanied only by the music of a pianist nearby. My day felt extravagant and cushy. My first holiday from motherhood made a lasting impression; now when the days and weeks overpower my patience and stamina, I make plans for another.

Taking regular breaks from one's children isn't a new

idea. Anne Morrow Lindbergh's classic 1955 book *A Gift from the Sea* urges mothers to take time away from their families to replenish themselves. On an island shore, Lindbergh collected shells and recorded timeless wisdom. "By and large, mothers and housewives are the only workers who do not have regular time off. They are the great vacationless class," she said. "If women were convinced that a day off or an hour of solitude was a reasonable ambition, they would find a way of attaining it."

In the spirit of Anne Morrow Lindbergh, take a hard look at your schedule, consult with those who support you, and plan a glorious day to enjoy all to yourself.

A Mother of *Your Own Design*

- By now, you understand your child-care options better than anyone. Summon the help of your partner, or thumb through your phone numbers. Plan your holiday right away.

- Use your motherhood journal to brainstorm getaway ideas. Choose a destination that appeals to you completely.

Week 37

Unlocked Memories
Revisiting Your Childhood

B ECOMING A MOTHER is like closing a circle; the pencil lifts off the page momentarily and begins again along the same arc. With childbirth, we start to retrace that circle. A montage of our earliest memories and experiences flickers involuntarily in our minds. The slide-show of our past guides our behavior as parents, away from or back again to our earliest experiences.

To enter motherhood without reflecting upon our own childhood would be like trying to ignore the prover-bial elephant in the room. Our past influences our par-enting decisions daily. We try to repeat the elements that shaped us positively, while avoiding those that affected us adversely. Measuring and weighing the present against the past is difficult to avoid; we all have some kind of model for parenting.

An early image that flashes in my mind is of my mother's youth and beauty. Her hair was long, dark, and blew across her face in the wind. She smiled often at my father. I remember watching her ironing his shirts in the afternoons while he was at work. She ate sunflower seeds in our backyard, dropping the shells from her fingertips into the grass. She chatted with neighbors on a park bench while I swung with friends at a playground on warm days. She had not yet finished college. She suspended her goals to take care of me, and eventually my sisters. She possessed a strong sense of duty. I knew that she loved me, and I also knew that she longed for more freedom during her days.

When I care for my children, I feel her fingerprints on my choices. I remember the way she washed my hair and the way she prepared dinner at night. When I was sick, she placed cool washcloths on my forehead and fed me crushed orange baby aspirin mixed with sugar and water on a spoon. Little things—like crushed baby aspirin—resurface in your mind when you become a mother. Without much thought, you'll do the same. It's second nature to kiss a bumped head and stroke soft curls. Of course there are other instincts, the ones we'd change if we could. We might feel impatient with the onset of temper tantrums, voicing anger that betrays our will.

We have little choice about our childhoods; we do have choices now. We step closer to our potential as mothers when we intersect our parents' best qualities with our own judgment and intuition. We're going to make mistakes sometimes. Becoming a mother of your own design is not easy. It's a constant dance with faith, one step toward the unknown and two steps back to the familiar.

A Mother of
Your Own Design

- Set aside an hour for writing in your motherhood journal. Think back on your childhood and record your earliest memories of your mother or father (or other prominent caregiver). Record memories in detail, the time of day, the color of scarf your mother wore. Can you remember your impressions as a child?

- Which memories do you cherish? Avoid? How do they influence you now as a mother?

SOLITUDE REVISITED

Claiming It for Yourself

A PSYCHOLOGIST FRIEND once told me that
she believed mothers who work outside the home
are generally more balanced than mothers who stay at
home. I've often wondered why. Is it because they have
more space to themselves during the day? Not being able
to think one's own thoughts is a huge challenge for a stay-
at-home mother who responds moment to moment to a
baby's needs. Dealing with drama all day long is also tough
on the emotions. It's impossible to escape crying, fits, and
fussiness. Then there are the physical demands of lifting,
nursing, and holding. At the end of the day, a mother who
has been at home often feels desperate for solitude.

Among my circle of friends who've chosen to mother
at home, the craving for solitude is universal and largely

unfulfilled. Why? The answer goes something like this: "I would like to have more time to myself, but I made the decision to stay at home. Anyway, I don't feel justified in paying for child care when I'm not working, and I'm not sure we could afford it anyway."

A friend of mine has two daughters, one three and one 10 months. Lately, when I talk with my friend, she doesn't laugh or seem to enjoy her life. She often tells me how hard her days are, and that her husband's career requires him to work until her children are in bed. She hasn't slept through the night in over a year, and hasn't been by herself for more than three hours since her second baby was born. She rarely hires a babysitter, and wonders why she's feeling depressed when she has been blessed with two healthy children.

Another mother told me, "I can't take it." She was referring to being at home for the first three weeks of her maternity leave. "I'm ready to go back to work now."

It's shocking to hear how unhappy mothers are at times, even when you've been there yourself. It's shocking because we might wonder how they can care well for their children when they're so unhappy themselves. Few people want to hear a woman say that she's tired of being a mother, not even another mother. Yet most women agree; staying at home with a baby is the most demanding job they've ever had.

Why is solitude so hard for mothers to justify? Solitude

is not a luxury to pine for. It can't be fit into a long weekend alone once a year. It is as essential to our children as the roof over their heads, and the food that we prepare for their bodies. If we are living healthy, well-balanced lives that include daily doses of solitude, we're full enough to nurture our children and enjoy doing so.

A Mother of
Your Own Design

- Our psyches desire a slice of solitude daily. It's difficult to know how much better you'll be as a mother if you haven't taken time for yourself before. Try it today or tomorrow. Go to bed and wake up an hour earlier. Incorporate some solitude into your exercise routine—walking by yourself in the evenings, or swimming laps at a local pool.

- If you don't have family members to assist you in watching the children, don't let the cost of an hour of babysitting get in the way. Reprioritize your spending to include some child care during the week. You need solitude more than Chinese takeout, pizza, or fast food. Look at the ways you spend your money. Giving up one dinner per week in a restaurant might pay for three hours of solitude.

Week 39

HOME

Calling Us to Ease

HOW WOULD I KNOW that the circumference of a banana breaks apart into perfect thirds if I didn't feed my little girl small bites of food? Or the way Goldfish crackers evoke baby giggles as they pour onto the tray of her highchair? Halved grapes and cut apples, perfect for grabbing, slide onto a plastic plate with colorful bunnies. A bottle with a tablespoon of milk lays abandoned on the floor of my kitchen, discarded with the discovery of blocks and satisfied thirst.

I cut, peel, and purée. She eats, drinks, and grows. Her healthy little body rushes around, stopping for a quick bite here and a little nibble there. Then she's off again to explore and conquer the space of our home. Under-explored corners await her touch. Handprints grace the first foot of every wall and window. Our house has become her home.

With children in our midst, the word *home* becomes luminous, a glowing residence in the dark night. A place of sanctuary, peace, and safety, a home transcends its bricks and mortar. The dwelling has spirit now, a loving atmosphere that embraces those who walk through the front door.

My grandfather once told me about the first time his father came to visit his home after he'd settled down and started his own family. My grandfather and grandmother had five children at the time. Their home was small for the size of their family, but my great-grandfather was taken with it. He told my grandfather in his native Dutch, "This house feels welcoming and good." His words were simple but familiar. We all know the feeling of a place that sets us at ease, invites us to be just who we are.

That's what I hope my home is to those who visit, and especially to those of us who abide here. There are times when I lament worn upholstery and smeared tabletops. But hours later I'll hear my husband and kids laughing under a quilt draped over the same chairs and tables—a makeshift fort more magical than its rumpled ingredients. A home always has utility beyond the scope of its walls and its contents, however modest they may be. The real ambiance is in the living, the day-to-day activities that skip from one room to the next.

I'm back in the kitchen again, serving raisins in a metal baby teacup. My daughter is overjoyed with her snack, dumping them out and picking them up one by one with newfound dexterity. She's at home, and happy.

A Mother of
Your Own Design

- List three homes that you've visited in which you felt comfortable. What makes them memorable?

- When you find yourself daydreaming over glossy home decorating magazines, remember that the spirit of our homes is reflected by its occupants more than by its décor.

Investment of Love

Living in a Troubled World

As I look out from the window of my baby's nursery, Canadian geese flap, squawk, and swim in a small pond beyond our yard. Our mornings and evenings are marked by their coming and going, wings skimming water and sky. Sometimes the birds share the sky with aircraft leaving and returning to a military base nearby. The remote roar of engines has become as familiar to my children's ears as their backyard geese.

Beyond our nursery window is nature. Beyond that is human nature, and an uncertain world that I cannot explain to my children no matter how old they are. I can name the geese, sky, clouds, trees, water, and airplanes. I cannot name our human tendency toward conflict. I shield them from it, turning off television images that belie their storybook illustrations. Hostility is a part of their world, as real as the dandelions that grow in our lawn. They love to pluck and blow on them, "making wishes" as they scatter the flowers' white fluffy seeds. They're too little to understand wishes, so I wish for them, for a peaceful life ahead.

Looking beyond our backyard, my hope as a mother wavers at times. Mothers live a dual existence—nurturing a world of innocence while trying to understand another world of malice. When news of war and destruction becomes a backdrop to living, it's difficult not to be afraid. The importance of family is more lucid to me now. Creating and maintaining the sanctuary of home is vital. Families, friends, and communities comfort and sustain us.

As mothers, we do everything in our power to soften the way for our children while gazing into a world that at times has no conscience. We create a safe beginning for them despite all that looms beyond the nest. We teach love in daily living, through simple acts of wiping away tired tears or kissing scraped knees. We dispel conflict in our own lives through caring for ourselves and for our marriages, fortifying the stability of our homes. We fight violence by modeling kindness, respecting life, and valuing peace.

American astronaut Rusty Schweickert once described his view of Earth from space. He said:

You look down there and you can't imagine how

many borders and boundaries you crossed again and again.... From where you see it, the thing is a whole and it's so beautiful.

Mothers possess a real power to transform the future. This first year of your baby's life could be the beginning of a new world, undivided and whole.

A Mother of
Your Own Design

- What are the ways that you can limit your exposure to images and reports of violence in your home? Andrew Weil, M.D., author of *Eight Weeks to Optimum Health*, recommends "news fasts," a day or more spent without reading the newspaper or watching television news. Limiting your exposure to disturbing reports can reduce stress, anger, fear, and anxiety.

- Peace starts with you. What are the ways that you can live more peacefully at home? In your community?

SUPPORTIVE WORDS

Longing for Encouragement

"AM I DOING A GOOD JOB?" you might ask yourself. This question appears like an apparition, haunting us when we feel tired or doubtful. How do we know for certain? We might long for quarterly reviews and performance bonuses, the nodding approval of a superior who acknowledges our hard work and dedication. Motherhood is more solitary than that. One day loops into another; there is no "end" to anticipate or celebrate. We tread an infinite passage.

I realized my longing for affirmation one day while at the pediatrician's office for my son's nine-month checkup. The pediatrician walked into our room and asked me a standard checklist of questions. How long is he sleeping at night? *Less than we'd like at times.* Is he eating well? *Is ignoring all green foods a problem?* How much milk does he drink in a day? *I'm not sure; he nurses about every four hours.*

The pediatrician looked up from his clipboard and smiled at me. Then he said something I'll never forget.

"I'm proud of you, Mrs. Braner, for still breastfeeding."

I could have wept. I think I did in the car as I drove home. His words of support were so novel to me, so foreign to my ears that when I heard them, I wanted to throw my arms around him.

How many of us go day in and day out without any encouragement? I know that my husband appreciates my work as a mother, but he is consumed as a parent in the same way that I am. We are both tangled in responsibility and care.

Love and a sense of duty might fuel us, but it's nice to occasionally hear praise from others. For some, our parents offer us support. And for others, we feel very much adrift on this raft, trying to steer our own course through these changing waters. Some days are smooth and others are stormy. It would be nice to lean on someone more experienced, who knows what we're going through and supports us along the way.

I've become friends with a few mothers whose children have grown and fled their nests. I value their insight, confidence, and I appreciate that they do not judge me as I share with them my awkward moments. They've become mentors to me—offering advice, soothing my worry, and complimenting my choices.

Parenting can be lonely at times, and it helps to reach out to others who understand. Mothers all struggle with the same questions. Instead of keeping to ourselves, let's reach out and ask for help. We might feel vulnerable admitting our uncertainty, but when we do, we just might find the encouragement we seek.

A Mother of
Your Own Design

- Who mentors you as a mother? You might have more than one. A mentor is someone who listens and encourages, not someone who questions and judges.

- If you're longing for more support in your life, think about the parents around you and in your community whom you respect. Is there a parent you admire whom you could invite to lunch? Taking the initiative to forge new friendships feels uncomfortable or even scary at first, but what do you have to lose?

WORKAHOLISM

Finding a Balance

IN OUR CULTURE, work is an acceptable alternative to almost anything. It's easy to bring home an assignment from the office, or if you stay at home, spend so much time mothering that you don't remember the last time you left the house by yourself. The risk of workaholism is real for many of us; employers usually revere it as if it were a virtue. Mothers who stay at home often feel the same. Many of us take pride in pushing ourselves to our outermost limits. In her book *The Artist's Way,* Julia Cameron says, "The phrase *I'm working* has a certain unassailable air of goodness and duty to it. The truth is, we are very often working to avoid ourselves, our spouses, our real feelings."

Are you perplexed by the question, "Am I working too much?" You're not alone. We're driven as mothers to nurture our children, and we're driven as women to learn and grow separately from our children. A mother who chooses to stay home shelves her freedom and interests for much of the time. A mother who chooses to return to the office entrusts some of her child's earliest and most formative development into the care of someone else. When we forgo one need for the other, we're left out of balance. Can a mother nurture her child from a place of lack for long? Not ideally. Are we satisfied as parents if we spend more time working than we do with our children? Not usually.

Workaholism is an extreme state, narrowly focused on one objective or activity. Just as an overworked stay-at-home mother might need to remember to think about herself more often, a mother with a demanding career might need to remember to think about her family and herself more often.

I hear your thoughts; you may not have any choice in how many hours you work at home or away. Ask yourself this question: Are you and your child adequately cared for during the day? If so, you're probably striking the right balance, which is the real question here. Working long hours every day, forfeiting time with yourself, your family, or both, even if you love your work, is not nurturing. It is one-dimensional.

Balancing our own needs with our child's needs is anything but easy. If possible, it takes the help of both mother and father—giving, taking, and remaining flexible. These choices don't have to fall on our shoulders alone. This question, "Am I working too much?" is one that only you can answer. Remaining conscious of your choices and honest about your reasons, you'll find the answer that's right for your family.

A Mother of *Your Own Design*

- Flexibility in the workplace has enabled parents the freedom to pursue their careers while spending more time with family. If you are looking for ways to spend more time at home, consider the possibility of job sharing or pursuing a more flexible schedule. Telecommuting or working from home can be a good alternative, but the line between work and family blurs easily. You also might miss the camaraderie of being in an office.

- If mothering is your full-time work and you rarely allow yourself time off, ask yourself why. Mothers sometimes harbor judgment for themselves and others when it comes to spending time away from their children. There is nothing wrong with pursuing your interests, professionally or otherwise. Your work as a mother is only enriched when you fulfill your needs as a woman.

A MOTHER'S PLAY

Enjoying It

WE WORK SO DILIGENTLY, but do we endeavor to enjoy motherhood as much as we wish to be good at it? Like any endeavor, it's nice to pause and take in the scenery. What's the use otherwise? Are we destined to be on a treadmill staring at the same wall every morning? Wouldn't it be nice to run outside for a change, watching life unfold with each new stride?

I awoke this morning to a baby's laughter. My husband lowered my daughter onto my chest as I was just opening my eyes. Her fuzzy pajamas tickled my nose, and she curled up beside me. Drowsy, I closed my eyes again and when I opened them, she was still staring at me smiling. Let's freeze time, cut out this moment, and paste it into a book of prized memories. I'd like instant access to it again, years or even days from now when I'm overworked and out of sorts.

Now we're at a playground, it's a September day, and we're enjoying our first taste of autumn. Blue skies and cooler temperatures have called many families from their homes, the din of play rising above the swings and slides. There's my son, climbing the stairs to the "big slide," a towering metal attraction that scares me more than it does him. His father is standing at the bottom of the stairs, giving him more freedom than his frightened mother ever would. And here's my daughter, for her first time, in a playground swing for toddlers. I pull back on her swing and then stand in front of her. "Eeeeooh!" she squeals with abandon as she sways back and forth, her curls dancing on the air.

Again, freeze this moment.

Although I'm certainly not always aware of it, I suspect every day with our children offers these treasures. If we could only see around the corner of our domestic duties and fatigue, we might reenter the playground and a world of wonder.

And how does that happen? We could remember to step back and take in the life unfolding in front of us. We might need to sit down and acknowledge ourselves for a job well done. We could take stock of our work as mothers, and tune into the joy of our accomplishments more often. With every turn in our children's development there is a similar turn in our own. These are triumphant times. Let's enjoy them.

A Mother of *Your Own Design*

- Make a list of the ways you've grown since becoming a mother. Make another list of the ways your child has grown since infancy. Tape them someplace visible in your home.

- For the next week, identify one accomplishment per day that makes you proud. Don't think too hard about this. Be proud of yourself for the small things— brushing baby teeth, serving nutritious snacks, or singing songs before bed.

WALK WITH THE WIND

Daydreaming and Nostalgia

I DON'T KNOW ABOUT YOU, but I'm feeling a bit weary of *Sesame Street* and nursery rhymes today. I'd like to walk with the wind, feel the freedom of a sunny day, and commune with a shady tree. I'm longing for spring, but winter beckons. It's sunny but cold, and my son can't get enough of Elmo and Ernie.

While PBS entertains, I reminisce unexpectedly about life prior to motherhood and marriage. Does nostalgia bubble up when life becomes too predictable? What is it about that time, with its near-empty refrigerator and untidy apartment, that I miss suddenly? Could it be the phone conversations with friends that extended well beyond a "decent hour"? Or the way my neighbor, a professional chef, invited me downstairs to sample an exotic creation?

Do I miss daydreaming about my future, then a wide unmarked canvas? Perhaps I miss living on the brink of discovering who I was.

Motherhood settles us. It gives us a map for our future, which feels comforting at times and confining at others.

Do you remember when you were more in touch with the edges in life, the sharp experiences that happen when you're open to everything? Did you meet new people while out with your girlfriends on Saturday nights? Did you pursue dreams of becoming a jazz club singer or an entrepreneur? Do you remember envisioning a vivid future while it was still fuzzy and forming? It was easier to walk the plank of hopes and dreams then. We had no choice. Uncertainty felt invigorating; it tested the limits of who we were. Those days were not always comfortable, and perhaps that's why I miss them. Pursuing the promise of ourselves is some of the most interesting and challenging work we can do.

We might have something to glean from our nostalgia when it emerges. The whispering Self might want to be remembered, appreciated, and realized. Our capacity for living is larger than we sometimes remember. Children have a way of polishing our edges; we might relinquish small details of ourselves without even realizing it. We're dedicated parents, so it happens willingly.

Our lives need some intricacy, spontaneity, and fun. Motherhood is an exercise in balance: your baby needs you and you need you. How can you open yourself up again to the pursuit of a new interest or at least some time each week for fun—dining out with friends or salsa dancing with your partner? Our spirits are still vibrant; our lives should sparkle a little too.

A Mother of
Your Own Design

- What memories have bubbled up into your thoughts lately? Are you feeling nostalgic for another time? What do you find alluring about it?

  - How can you encourage the esteemed qualities of your younger self to reemerge?

THE DESERT

Creating an Oasis

IT'S NOT UNCOMMON or even rare that I hear from a friend who's having a bad day as a mother. "He hasn't taken a nap all day, and he won't let me put him down," she says. "My arms are killing me. He nurses constantly. I'm on my last leg."

We've all had days like these, minutes that stretch into vast deserts. Will we ever find civilization again? Not until we have a moment to breathe. When that oasis appears, if we don't rest long enough or drink enough water, civilization disappears again like a mirage on the horizon. I suspect thousands of us are trudging circles through the same desert, but somehow we never run into each other.

Let's glimpse at some indicators of our well-being before losing ourselves in a sandstorm. Look at your bank account;

is it balanced? Glance at the gas and oil gauges in your car; are they filled? Is your refrigerator full? When was the last time you ate a healthy meal or drank a glass of water? Have you made love with your husband lately? What falls by the wayside when life gets busy?

Restoring sanity after a difficult day requires tending to our needs, halting everything else and asking the question, "What do I want?" You might wash your hair and paint your toenails red. You might find yourself at the video store in search of a comedy. With a few laughs and clean hair, we're bound to feel better.

What if we weaved a few of these things into our day when possible? It's more difficult to keep a baby busy while making a salad for lunch, but we're worth the extra effort. We could keep a cold pitcher of filtered water in the fridge for ourselves during the day. We might even drop a few lemon and lime slices into the pitcher in the morning, or before we go to bed at night. Keeping a running list of groceries to buy makes it easier to keep the kitchen stocked with wholesome and fresh foods. We could pay bills as they arrive, avoiding late fees and stacks of paper on the kitchen counter. These tasks, seemingly mundane, are what make our days manageable and even enjoyable. Our homes serve more than our children; they should serve us too. A bad day is sometimes a symptom of our own neglect—inattentiveness to our body, heart, mind, or spirit.

A Mother of
Your Own Design

- When caring for yourself seems like more work than pleasure, it's time to pause. At that instant, come up with three nice things that you can do for yourself. Whether you feel inspired or not, do them over the course of the day. Notice how you feel afterward.

- Kindness is a habit that we must consciously cultivate for our children and ourselves. When we're kind to ourselves, a bad day softens.

Week 46

Money

Using It Wisely

MONEY FACTORS INTO motherhood in many ways. The financial requirements of parenting hit us before our children are even born. We shell out a small fortune to dress and stock a nursery. Who knew that minute details, like diaper disposal, would be a financial decision? Do I buy the trashcan with "odorless" storage and removal, or do I recycle my grocery bags and walk outside more often? Having a baby is a lesson in merchandising and self-control. We want the best for our children, so it's easy to believe that they "need" a diaper wipe warmer or the name-brand diapers on the shelves.

When luxuries are disguised as necessities, it's difficult to make wise choices concerning our money and parenting. It's facile to begin nodding with the marketing brain of retailers who try to pad their pockets with our good intentions. The media feeds our parental expectations. The pressure to conform and "to have" is formidable. We might even question ourselves if we can't afford or refuse to purchase a popular "learning toy" for our ten-month-old.

Living in a society that values "things," we sometimes forget what our children need most of all—us. If we invested as much time and money into our future and ourselves as we do into things, what kind of parents would we be? The way we spend or save our money is a significant statement about what we value. I personally don't value baby clothes over a college education, yet the call of a tiny designer periwinkle-striped cardigan will catch me off guard. Suddenly I'm imagining my daughter admired by others, and I in turn feel admired as her mother. Why am I drawn to packaging over content? Invested over eighteen years, the value of that sweater might pay for a semester's worth of schoolbooks. Today, it would pay for five hours of babysitting—enough for a couple dates with my husband—or a week's worth of aerobics classes. The choice to decline a beautiful but expensive sweater signifies more than financial discretion. It means that I value my daughter and myself as a mother, with or without the stamp of name-brand approval.

We encourage independent thinking in our children by thinking independently ourselves. Our choices might be different from other parents', but they'll be our own. If you find yourself weighing decisions about things to buy for your child, or yourself, look hard at your rationale. Who cares most about them? How would the future value of that money serve your family down the road?

Financial advisor and author Suze Orman states "the first law of money" in her book *The Courage to Be Rich.* She writes, "People first. Then money. Then things." Expenses pile up quickly when bringing up children, but we have more choices than we realize when it comes to our money. The richness of motherhood has little to do with our bank account balances, and everything to do with how much of ourselves we invest along the way. When we keep this perspective, we're less likely to fill our homes with the will of advertisers. And not surprisingly, we're likely to live more abundantly.

A Mother of
Your Own Design

- If you're feeling financially frazzled, take control of your money. Talk to a financial advisor, or read a book about managing your money. Be as responsible with your income as you are with your child.

- Advertisers target not only parents but also very young children. Shield yourself from their efforts as much as possible. It's easier to resist spending when you avoid the temptation.

THE *L*URE OF *E*FFICIENCY
Succumbing to the Temptation of Tupperware

SOMETHING ABOUT motherhood, probably its flurry of activity, renders many of us helpless to daydreams of efficiency. Retailers seem to know this. They target mothers with catalogs of products designed to contain, clean, simplify, and systematize. We all know there are no easy solutions to the demands of motherhood. We might drop them in our recycling bins, vowing not to be persuaded by catalogs containing tidy monochromatic kitchens and pantries. I personally believed that I had inoculated myself from their promises of a better life. That is, until *it* arrived.

There it was one afternoon, resting in the corner of my mailbox in a crisp yellow envelope. An invitation, I thought, pulling it out from the catalogs and bills. I wondered who might be having a party? I carved a careful opening with my letter opener and read the first line on the card:

You're Invited to a Tupperware Party

This was a moment that I never thought I'd see. My mother's olive-green plastic canisters with clear airtight lids flashed before me. There we were in the kitchen, earning my Girl Scout cooking badge as we baked cookies and pies. Then I remembered her banana-colored orange peeler, a Tupperware icon in the kitchen. I owned nothing of the sort. And now, twenty years later, I was being summoned to a gathering of mothers keen on efficiency and culinary innovation. I felt obliged; how could I turn it down when my own childhood flickered with memories of hot summers and Tupperware juice-pops?

So I went and watched, mesmerized as a parade of kitchen gadgets—whirling, peeling, flipping, storing, and decorating—marched before me. I was hypnotized by the enthusiasm in the room. That's when I saw it for the first time, a three-piece hi-tech stacking system that cooks an entire dinner in the microwave in 30 minutes. I salivated at the potential. Visions of fast nutritious nightly dinners danced in my head. I knew this was the answer to my cooking woes, the solution that would change my maternal life. I didn't blink at the price. I signed the check and waited for it to be delivered two weeks later.

Thankfully my new cookware came with its own recipes. I chopped, prepared, and stored ingredients in the morning to be ready for my first run. And it performed. I tried it again the next day, and it worked again. I was still cooking, mind you, just in a hi-tech cranberry-colored container. I'm sure that there are other mothers who've perfected this culinary microwave skill, whose families have tasted a lot of bang for their bucks, but I fizzled out after the first week. I missed baked lasagna and crispy casseroles. I was a Tupperware dropout.

Now, I know that I'm not alone in my optimism for an easier way. But maybe there's something to be said for just doing the work, with all of the time, mess, and care it takes. So what if we serve grilled-cheese sandwiches for dinner on the nights we're pinched for time? Does this really say anything about us other than our affection for warm melted cheese sandwiches?

A Mother of
Your Own Design

- List the items that you've purchased in the last year with the hope of increasing your efficiency at home. How many of them have succeeded?

- Are your expectations for efficiency realistic? What's fueling them?

Week 48

Authenticity

Living Your Own Truth

Perhaps the one true occupation we have while we stroll this Earth is to discover who we are, and after that, to live in our bodies bravely. We don't come closer to ourselves by pushing away the pull of our soul. No one denies the call of Spirit happily for long; like a birdsong it wakes us in the morning and accompanies us throughout the day. It fades only with our awareness, and returns with the same.

Motherhood is one facet of our existence. To extend it to the sole reason we walk the Earth denies the whole of who we are. When we deny parts of ourselves in order to parent, our efforts are anemic, lacking key nutrients that feed our children and ourselves. Tune in and hear the song of your soul. Where is it leading you?

Artists, musicians, and writers mingle with their songs—on the canvas, in a waltz, or on the page. Their work is to open themselves to the highest call of their being, the one that embraces and reflects all of their experiences. A call to compose a sonata does not mask the call to love a child. It magnifies it, brings it closer to us, enables us to embrace motherhood.

We know authentic choices when we see them. My friend recently spent her spare time in a dance studio, choreographing and honing her talent to audition for a university dance program. Her peers in the program will be nearly half her age, but her passion and skill are the qualities that matter. She also happens to be the doting mother of three boys. Her sons could not describe their mother without also describing her love of dance. It becomes their love too, and a reference point for living the lives to which they will be called eventually.

We teach our children in many ways. We teach them with words and silence. We teach them through joy and sorrow, through sacrifice and commitment. We teach them with our choices.

There's a known path we can walk as mothers. It's paved, flanked with road signs and people who will tell us if we've taken a wrong turn. It's safe, and we might enjoy its predictability. While we walk, the trees beside the road bend toward us in the wind. The birds sing to us from nests in those branches, beckoning us to leave our easy stride and ramble along an undiscovered trail. We might be afraid to listen; there is some risk in parting from the known. But the self will not be denied for long; our happiness and well-being suffer otherwise. We need only to summon some courage, and take a few steps toward those notes on the wind.

A Mother of
Your Own Design

- What do you fear most about yourself? Your desire for a better relationship? The desire to quit your job? Sometimes our fear cloaks deep insight. Find a way to examine your feelings safely, perhaps in your motherhood journal or in a conversation with a trusted confidant or counselor. Listen to the urgings of your heart.

- What are some small ways that you can move in the direction of the life you feel called to live?

Holidays Anew

Living in the Moment

How many years did you walk through a shopping mall during the holidays, hurrying past the long line of parents and children waiting to sit on Santa's lap? You might have held your breath as you burrowed through crowds, determined to make it to as many stores as possible. Did you see the lighted snowflakes hanging from the ceilings? Did you listen to the student choir serenading you with carols full of hope, goodwill, and peace?

For my son's first Christmas, I stood in Santa's line with many other new mothers and fathers, our babies tucked in arms or strollers. Life-sized red and green candy canes flanked the entrance to Santa's den. Parents peered around winter coats and shopping bags, eagerly trying to catch a peek of the white bearded man dressed in red velvet.

The elves and Mrs. Claus worked the crowd, cooing at babies and handing out peppermint sticks and order forms. It's possible that we were the most cheerful adults in the mall, as though we were meeting Santa for the first time. Then suddenly, as if led by the Ghost of Christmas Past, I saw my old self stride past me. She sighed, checked her watch a couple times, and darted into a store and out of my view. She didn't bother looking our way. Her hurried pace and fixed gaze made me realize how much my son had opened my eyes again to life.

I seldom glance at my watch these days. In fact, I usually forget I'm even wearing one. "Having a baby is living in the eternal now. Having a baby means caring intensely about the stage you're going through, while forgetting everything that happened more than a week ago," says mother and writer Alisa Kwitney about the timelessness and novelty of maternal life in her essay "The Eternal Now." Children reawaken our senses, allowing us to share their joy in experiencing a single moment. So many moments call to us if we will only listen. May this holiday season rekindle your awareness of the simple pleasures in life.

A Mother of
Your Own Design

- Don't be persuaded by the celebration of your baby's first winter holidays to bake ten dozen cookies, decorate the entire house, and host a holiday dinner for twenty relatives. Enjoy this time by choosing selectively which traditions you'll honor. Keeping it simple will allow you to celebrate wholeheartedly.

- Select some spiritual texts to read during this time, turning your attention away from the more commercial aspects of the season and tuning into the quiet blessings of a winter's day.

A Sense of Place

Driving with Family

APPROACHING MY son's first birthday, I noticed an expression on his face that I've come to love. Driving home from dinner with friends, my son gazed placidly at the night sky through his window. He was content in his car seat, his parents nearby and familiar songs playing on the stereo. His expression revealed a sense of place in our little car, in our presence. And for the first time, I noticed what he had come to rely on—the comfortable aura of our family. I remember that backseat security as a child. The only difference was that then my parents were steering; now my husband and I were behind the wheel.

Although it had been more than twenty years since I'd ridden in my parents' backseat, I traveled deeper into adulthood that night. Having children draws us back to family life again, to road trips, playgrounds, neighborhoods, and pizza dinners with friends. There is a breaking away from "I" and a concerted effort toward "we."

I'm relieved to wake up to giggles and bottles, even small puddles of milk on my sheets in the morning. I like rubber ducks in my bathtub and diaper wipes in my glove compartment. I'll gladly skip to a fine restaurant with my girlfriends for a night out, but I have learned to dine on bagels, yogurt, dry cereal, and apple juice. Nightly nursery rhymes, lullabies, and prayers fill our home. Dishes fill the sink and toys fill the living room. Between the furniture and in spite of the clutter, small happy feet scamper through our home all day long.

This time that we inhabit, with all of its busyness and duty, comes only once. I try to remember that when I've straightened too many rooms and wiped too many runny noses. Then in the car, with the moon lighting the treetops around us, the whirl of our day was forgotten. A song ended softly and the hum of the road filled the air. My son sighed, asleep in his car seat. As I glanced again at him, I saw in his contentment the clear reflection of my own.

A Mother of
Your Own Design

- In your motherhood journal, describe the aura of your family. How does it differ or compare to that of your family of origin?

- Busy living aside, are you content with this time of your life? If not, what do you need to do for yourself in order to enjoy it more?

A BONNET

Preserving Small Treasures

A SMALL BONNET HANGS from a peg in my baby's nursery. Its strings dangle down the wall, untouched in months. Made from white eyelet, it represents all of my dreams about motherhood. It marks the time before birth, that pregnant hopeful time when bonnets and booties lay neatly in newly papered drawers. How long ago it seems, readying myself for the hospital on the eve of my son's arrival. I feel such fondness for that time, and thankfully, I revisit it with every friend's new pregnancy.

"I heard the baby's heartbeat today and I was overcome with tears," Tanya shared over the phone. Her joy bubbles up from the receiver, and I remember my own joy in hearing my children's heart beat for the first time.

"We're shopping for cribs now," reports Marya. "Does yours have slats on the bottom or springs?" she asks, trying to ensure adequate sleep standards for her baby-on-the-way. I don't tell her that my babies wanted to sleep with me during the first few months. Instead, we come up with a list of furniture stores that might carry white sleigh bed-style cribs. I envision her son's nursery—comfortable, warm, and waiting for his arrival. Every child should be so lucky.

We anticipate our children with such hope, and when they're born, we match our anticipation with great effort. We try hard and learn quickly, swimming on instinct after plunging into the water. Is there any other time in our adult lives when we learn as much about ourselves?

I've conceded finally; I've begun boxing up baby clothes that are too small. The pale blue overalls in which I've dressed my son dozens of times are going to be sitting in a crowded attic. My daughter's pink dress with the white sailor collar will have to be packed away too. The stuffy room above our garage hardly seems like a worthy place for these soft treasures. With every shirt that I fold, I tuck away memories. Good-bye blue shoes, the ones that my son wore on his first plane ride to visit his grandparents. Good-bye white cardigan, the one my daughter wore out-side on chilly autumn days.

The drawers and closet are emptier now, ready to collect new clothes and memories. Before closing the box,

I reach toward my children's first bonnet still hanging on its peg. My fingers brush the fabric and run along the edge of the ruffle, but I cannot lift it from the peg. I've decided to leave it hanging, a reminder of my first blush of motherhood.

A Mother of
Your Own Design

- How will you remember these days? Baby clothes are tactile reminders of this time. Choose one or two items that hold special significance to you, stow them away with your motherhood journal, baby book, and photo albums.

- If you feel sadness in letting go of your child's babyhood, spend an afternoon ruminating about the past year. Watch family videos; look through photos and cards. Step away and reflect upon this time, which is indeed passing quickly.

Week 52

A *New Day*

Loving Your Child and Yourself

I HAD A REVELATION today. In spite of all my efforts as a mother, my children will not wake up one morning and be perfect. Just as I will never "arrive" as a mother, they will never "arrive" as children. My work is to companion them on their journeys, guiding, loving, and teaching them to love themselves along the way. Maybe that's what our responsibility is to ourselves, too, as parents—loving ourselves at our best, in uncertainty, and in spite of flat-out failure.

Trying to raise civil, kind, confident, loving children is no small task. They're learning. We're teaching and learning.

At the end of the first year, our babies have reached beyond the nest of our arms. They're mobile, discovering and learning on their own. Babyhood drifts into the toddler years in the blink of time's eye. With their burgeoning independence, we're asking new questions, and wondering if we ever really needed all of those receiving blankets stacked in the hall closet. I carried my daughter in a front pack for months, running errands and cooking dinner with her head against my heart, but the vividness of that time has already begun to fade. The first year of motherhood dilutes like watercolor; the soft essence of experience hovers in memory. Sleeplessness probably blurs some of our recollections, challenges, and triumphs. But that's okay. We've made it through.

We've made it through colic, diaper rash, fevers, and fatigue. We've witnessed their first smile, grasp, and word. We've watched their minds unfurl, discovering us, the world around them, and finally themselves.

Our children need us. They need us to be their mothers, to hold their hands when they're scared and hug them when they're crying. They need us to dance with them in the afternoon and kiss their wet cheeks after a bath. Children love to hear stories read to them at night, to be encouraged to turn pages and point to pictures.

When we have enough time for ourselves, we're not distracted. Willingly, we give ourselves over to motherhood. We're not waiting impatiently for our partners to take over, nor looking forward to naptime. We're able to enjoy our children.

I recognize when my daughter wants more time discovering the soft grass that twines the red brick path in our backyard. She's fascinated, enthralled with running her fingers along both textures. She giggles as the tips of her fingers meet the top of the grass. I see her curiosity, the ecstasy of her discovery. I see because I am there wholeheartedly. I wonder how many of these moments have passed me by, like sand through a sieve, because I didn't have the presence of mind to notice. In order to see, we must step away sometimes. When we don't attend to our needs, our days cloud over. We're mired in details, watching the clock and waiting to breathe.

When we return, the clouds evaporate, the sun shines brightly, and the day is clear. I see my children's faces and their spirits. I see their eyes shining up at me, looking to me to help them interpret their world. And today, I reveal to them a contented hopeful place. To be fulfilled and content as a mother might be the greatest gift that you give your child.

A Mother of
Your Own Design

- Spend fifteen undivided minutes watching and listening to your child. You can observe much in just a little amount of time. Notice his joy in your presence.

- Celebrate your first year as a mother in a meaningful way. Compose a poem to recite at your child's first birthday party, or spend an afternoon by yourself reading over your motherhood journal. Recognize and celebrate your growth as a woman and mother.

Resource Guide

BOOKS TO SUPPORT YOU

Motherhood

Big Purple Mommy: Nurturing Our Creative Work, Our Children, and Ourselves by Coleen Hubbard. The Berkeley Publishing Group, Berkeley, 2001.

The Blue Jay's Dance: A Birth Year by Louise Erdrich. HarperPerennial, New York, 1995.

Child of Mine: Original Essays on Becoming a Mother (includes "The Eternal Now" by Alisa Kwitney) edited by Christina Baker Kline. Dell Publishing, New York, 1997.

Diary of a Baby by Daniel Stern, M.D. Basic Books, New York, 1990.

A Gift from the Sea by Anne Morrow Lindbergh.
Pantheon Books, New York, 1955.

*I Wish Someone Had Told Me: A Realistic Guide to Early
Motherhood* by Nina Barrett. Academy Chicago
Publishers, Chicago, 1997.

The Myth of the Perfect Mother: Parenting without Guilt
by Jane Swigart, Ph.D. Contemporary Books,
Chicago, 1991.

*Sleeping Through the Night: How Infants, Toddlers and
Their Parents Can Get a Good Night's Sleep* by Jodi A.
Mindell, Ph.D. HarperCollins, New York, 1997.

Solve Your Child's Sleep Problems by Richard Ferber,
M.D. Simon & Schuster, New York, 1986.

Creativity

The Artist's Way: A Spiritual Path to Higher Creativity by
Julia Cameron. Tarcher/Putnam, New York, 1992.

Literary Escape

Driving Over Lemons: An Optimist in Andalucía by
Chris Stewart. Sort of Books, London, 1999.

Encore Provence by Peter Mayle. Knopf, New York,
1999.

Under the Tuscan Sun by Frances Mayes. Broadway
Books, New York, 1996.

Health and Well-Being

Anatomy of the Spirit: The Seven Stages of Power and Healing by Caroline Myss. Harmony Books, New York, 1996.

The Courage to Be Rich: Creating a Life of Material and Spiritual Abundance by Suze Orman. Riverhead Books, New York, 1999.

Eight Weeks to Optimum Health: A Proven Program for Taking Full Advantage of Your Body's Natural Healing Power by Andrew Weil, M.D. Fawcett Books, New York, 1998.

Take Time for Your Life by Cheryl Richardson. Broadway Books, New York, 1998.

The Woman's Comfort Book by Jennifer Louden. HarperSanFrancisco, San Francisco, 1992.

MUSIC TO INSPIRE YOU

Amadeus, Wolfgang Amadeus Mozart (Soundtrack)

As Time Goes By, Tuck & Patti

The Cello Suites, Johan Sebastian Bach (Performed by Yo Yo Ma)

Chant, Gregorian chants (Performed by the Benedictine Monks of Santo Domingo De Silos)

A Day Without Rain, Enya

Fantasies & Delusions, Billy Joel (Joel's first classical album; performed by Richard Joo)

Illumina, selected artists (Sacred music exploring the
  theme of light; performed by the Choir of Clare
  College, Cambridge)
Immortal Beloved, Ludwig van Beethoven (Soundtrack)
On a Starry Night, selected artists (Lullabies from
  around the world)
*Singable Songs for the Very Young: Great with a Peanut
  Butter Sandwich,* Raffi

WEB SITES TO ASSIST YOU

www.allaboutmoms.com
  All About Moms offers helpful advice and information for new mothers. Provides message boards.
www.lalecheleague.org
  La Leche League is an international nonprofit
  organization dedicated to providing education, information, support, and encouragement to women
  who want to breastfeed.
www.myria.com
  An online magazine created to support, inform, and
  encourage women who are mothers.
www.midlifemother.com
  Mid-Life Mother offers discussion on mid-life pregnancy and parenting.

www.nomotc.org

The National Organization of Mothers of Twins Clubs site supports parents of twins and higher-order multiples.

www.parentsplace.com

An extensive parenting resource center that also provides bulletin boards, chat rooms, and weekly special features.

www.20ishparents.com

The 20ish Parents site addresses issues relevant to mothers in their twenties.

ACKNOWLEDGMENTS

THE INKLING OF A BOOK comes long before a proposal is written and agents are consulted. For me, the courage to express myself through writing emerged in the caring company of family and friends. My grandparents, artist Henry John Groen and poet Geneviève St. Cyr, were the first to see me as a writer when my words were still young and clumsy. In their presence, my love of language blossomed. I owe my perseverance to my father, Jay Groen, who has taught me to follow my dreams. My mother, Margaret Groen, has given me a steady foundation from which I feel confident to stretch and grow as a mother and a writer.

Thank you to my agent, Katie Boyle, for being the angel who believed in this book and found it a home.

Thank you to my editor, Heather McArthur, and executive editor Leslie Berriman for helping me to sharpen my focus, allowing me to write the book that was in my heart. Thank you also to my copyeditor, Pam Suwinsky, to my production editor, Jill Rogers, and to everyone at Conari who designed and promoted this book.

Many others have supported me along the way, reading unfinished passages or listening to me talk about unfinished passages. Thank you to Daphne Stevens, a wise mentor whose encouraging words always arrived in the nick of time. Thank you also to my dear friend Lydia Schindler, whose loyalty and care keep me afloat. Thank you to Holly Bradshaw, Jodi Dixon, Jean Marriott, Pam Nault, Kelly Randall, Denise Sharpe, Ellis Stroud, Michele and John Twigg. Thank you to my generous and loving in-laws, Roger and Karen Braner. Thank you to Mark Bergel for introducing me to the concept of holism years ago. Thank you also to the Rev. Dan Edwards and St. Francis Church for your quiet and enriching presence in my life.

Finally, none of this would have been possible without the support of my family, especially my husband, Roger, who believes it is his duty to nurture and care for our children as much as it is mine. My children, Matthew and Sophia, teach me daily about the breadth of love; their presence in my life has transformed me.

For all of you, I am grateful.

ABOUT THE AUTHOR

LISA GROEN BRANER is a mother and writer committed to weaving hope, courage, and soul into her work at home and on the page. Braner has served as editor of an international magazine and several newsletters, and has published articles on motherhood, parenting, and health. She lives in Georgia with her husband and their two children.

For more information about Lisa Groen Braner, you may visit her Web site at lgbraner.com.

To Our Readers

CONARI PRESS PUBLISHES books on topics ranging
from spirituality, personal growth, and relationships to
women's issues, parenting, and social issues. Our mission
is to publish quality books that will make a difference in
people's lives—how we feel about ourselves and how we
relate to one another. We value integrity, compassion, and
receptivity, both in the books we publish and in the way
we do business.

As a member of the community, we dedicate a por-
tion of our proceeds from certain books to charitable causes,
and continually look for new ways to use natural resources
as wisely as possible.

Our readers are our most important resource, and we value your input, suggestions, and ideas about what you would like to see published. Please feel free to contact us, to request our latest book catalog, or to be added to our mailing list.

Conari Press
An imprint of Red Wheel/Weiser, LLC
P.O. Box 612
York Beach, ME 03910-0612
800-423-7087
www.conari.com